Reza Torkzadeh's excellent t
personal injury law in Califor
accident would benefit enormously from reading

a masterful job at making difficult legal concepts accessible to a wide
audience.

—Erwin Chemerinsky

Our society benefits when we all know about our rights. *Accidents Happen*
by Reza Torkzadeh and Allen P. Wilkinson is a clear and informative
guide for every consumer who wishes to learn more about the system of
tort law—the law of wrongful injuries—in California.

—Ralph Nader

Reza's book is well tailored to people who are involved—or considering whether to get involved—in lawsuits. It's a solid overview of what
to expect and how the civil system and law work. The book is clear,
concise, and to the point on every topic. It's a welcome resource that
bridges the gap between citizens and the legal world. Since the system
belongs to the citizens, they have every right to understand it. With this
book, they will.

—David Ball

In my years on the bench, I saw too many individuals with personal injury
claims who came into court without any idea of what to expect. To enter
any sort of legal proceeding without being acquainted with the legal process is to do oneself a disservice. *Accidents Happen* is an excellent first
step to consider if you wish to proceed with making a claim.

—Hon. (ret.) Joseph S. Biderman

If you're wondering if you have a solid personal injury claim or how to
effectively monitor your lawyer's work, I recommend you run, don't walk,
to your nearest e-book seller and purchase and read this book authored
by a highly competent personal injury litigation lawyer you can rely on! I
know him AND trust him!

—Hon. (ret.) Judge William Sheffield

Most injury victims end up getting confused, intimidated by the scope and scale of the process and frustrated by the delays and what feels like a huge run around. *Accidents Happen* gives you, the victim, the knowledge and background you need to keep the legal system from pushing you around. Getting informed has never been easier."

Being informed about your rights can be the difference between winning and losing your injury case. *Accidents Happen* explains your rights like no other book can, and does so with the care and coherence you'd expect from a close friend.

Being injured can often feel like the system is rigged against you. The only way to turn the tables back your way and to make sure you are in control is to be informed. Torkzadeh and Wilkinson give you all the tools you need to level the field with this amazing book. I urge you to read it so you can be in charge of your case.

—Wendy R. Fleishman, Esq.

Unfortunately, the system is stacked against the accident victim. Knowledge and preparation are important tools to level the field. *Accidents Happen* provides the reader with the background and information necessary to navigate and understand the legal process.

—Yvonne Flaherty, Esq.

ACCIDENTS HAPPEN

ACCIDENTS HAPPEN

A CONSUMER'S GUIDE TO THE
PERSONAL INJURY AND WRONGFUL DEATH SYSTEM

REZA TORKZADEH, ESQ.

ALLEN P. WILKINSON, ESQ.

PIGEON
LAKE
PUBLISHING

Copyright © 2017 by Reza Torkzadeh and Allen P. Wilkinson

All rights reserved. No part of this publication may be reproduced, stored in a retrieval system, or transmitted, in any form or by any means, electronic, mechanical, photocopying, recording or otherwise, without the express prior permission of Pigeon Lake Publishing.

www.pigeonlakepublishing.com

Published 2017 by Pigeon Lake Publishing

Printed in the United States of America

ISBN: 978-0-692-85483-9

Cover design by Pigeon Lake Publishing

Cover image provided by Shutterstock

DISCLAIMER

Every attempt has been made to ensure the accuracy of the law and what you should do in the event you are injured or a loved one is killed by another person's actions, defective product, or other cause.

This book does not offer legal advice and will never replace the consultation of a licensed attorney who has the experience and resources to properly handle your claim.

The materials in this book have been prepared for informational purposes only and should not be construed as, or relied upon as, legal advice or legal opinion on any specific facts or circumstances.

These materials do not, and are not, intended to constitute legal advice. Every situation is unique to the facts of the case and the law that applies. Readers should not rely or act upon any information contained in this book without first consulting a personal injury lawyer experienced in the area of the law involved.

By reading this book, you are not establishing an attorney-client relationship with the authors.

CONTENTS

Foreword for the Second Edition xi

Foreword from the First Edition. xv

Introduction xvii

A Note on Negligence and Tort Law. xix

PART I: WHOSE FAULT IS IT?

1. Determining Responsibility 3

2. What If Both of You Were at Fault? 5

PART II: HOW MUCH IS MY CASE WORTH?

3. Damages Recoverable in a Personal Injury Case 9

4. Damages Recoverable in a Wrongful Death Case 12

5. How Lawyers Determine the Value of Your Case 17

PART III: BEFORE YOU SPEAK TO A LAWYER

. . . . 21

PART IV: WORKING WITH YOUR ATTORNEY

6 Finding the Right Attorney 33

7 The Contingency Fee Agreement 36

PART V: HOW A CASE PROCEEDS THROUGH
      THE JUSTICE SYSTEM

8. Before Filing a Lawsuit 41

9. Taking the Case to Trial 44

PART VI: TYPES AND EXAMPLES OF
      COMMON ACCIDENTS

10. Automobile Accidents 53

11. Municipal Transportation (Mass Transit) Accidents . 65

12. Large Truck Accidents 71

13. Train Accidents and Railroad Crossing Accidents . . . 82

14. Motorcycle Accidents 92

15. Bicycling Accidents 97

16. Pedestrian Accidents 103

17. Boating and Personal Watercraft Accidents 106

18. "Slip and Falls" and "Trip and Falls" 111

19. Elevator and Escalator Injuries. 117

20. Dog Bites and Attacks 125

21. Defective Products 130

22. Medical Malpractice 137

23. Amusement Parks and Traveling Carnival Rides . . . 141

24. Recreational and Spectator Sports 151

25. Aviation Law. 165

26. Cruise Ship Liability 182

PART VII: INJURIES AND DAMAGES

27. Whiplash and Soft-Tissue Injuries 195

28. Broken Bones 197

29. Spinal Cord Injuries 201

30. Traumatic Brain Injuries 207

31. Burn Injuries 214

32. Amputations 223

33. Psychological Injuries 229

34. Pain and Suffering 232

35. Damage to Your Vehicle and Its Contents 237

PART VIII: THE CASE AGAINST TORT REFORM

. . . . 241

PART IX: THE PAST, PRESENT AND FUTURE

36. The "Hot Coffee Lady" and "Frivolous Lawsuits 249

37. Ford's Pinto Fiasco and Defective Products 252

38. Changes to the Law 255

39. A Quickly Approaching and Unclear Future 261

AFTERWORD 265

ABOUT THE AUTHORS 267

INDEX 269

FOREWARD FOR THE SECOND EDITION

Nearly six years ago, we released the First Edition of Accidents Happen. We are extremely proud of the book and humbled by the response from our readers.

At the outset, we agreed that our goal was to get as many of our books as possible into the hands of those who needed it the most. I'm proud to say that since the release of the First Edition, we donated nearly 5,000 hard copies to consumers across the country, developed a free interactive version on our website, and made sure that Amazon/Kindle, iTunes, and other platforms made the book available to anyone who wanted a copy.

We will continue to work towards our goal of getting as many copies of this Second Edition as we can into the hands of those who are up against a powerful corporate defendant that has unlimited resources and will stop at nothing to keep you from obtaining justice.

Every day, I watch insurance companies and their armies of lawyers fight to keep injured victims and their families from receiving insurance benefits they are rightfully owed. I watch as these insurance companies spend billions of dollars every year to support candidates for elected office and organizations like the Chamber of Commerce. These politicians, judges, and special interest groups support and successfully enact anti-consumer laws designed to protect the insurance companies and their profits, all at the expense of the consumer. They do this under the guise of "Tort Reform."

These very powerful companies take pride in bullying, intimidating, and forcing the same people who trust them to take settlements significantly less than what is actually deserved and owed. Often times pennies on the dollar.

I describe the insurance companies as the modern day Goliath.

The entire insurance industry business model is to charge the highest possible premiums to the trusting public and then pay out as little as possible—even if it means spending millions of dollars on lawyers and expenses to keep you from being adequately compensated.

The way to fight these insurance companies is to be armed with the tools, information, and resources necessary to make what in many situations may be the most important decision of your life. We hope to achieve that with this book.

I have represented people from all walks of life. I once represented a homeless man who was struck by a car while crossing the street. I've represented members of our government, musicians, actors, and business owners who were harmed by others. I've represented families who have lost loved ones in accidents and by dangerous products or hazardous conditions on roadways against some of the world's most powerful companies.

I have spent countless hours with parents who have lost a child, spouses who have lost their life partners, and children who have lost a parent. Each and every time, the pain is still the same for me. It never goes away and I don't think it ever will.

The unthinkable situation that one's life can be so catastrophically altered in an instant is one of the harsh realities of life.

One's right to trial by a jury of one's peers is the only way that the average person can hold accountable a corporate defendant who has unlimited resources, wealth, and an army of lawyers to protect its profits.

In our society, there is nowhere else where the voice of twelve individuals carry such tremendous power. The ability of a jury to hold multi-billion dollar corporations accountable for their actions, to protect the community from future harm, and to change the lives of those who have been harmed cannot be done in any setting other than a courtroom in a civil trial. It is the greatest gift and foundation of our justice system. It is what makes our justice system (while not perfect) the greatest one on the planet.

Reza Torkzadeh

FOREWORD FROM THE FIRST EDITION

I am a consumer. Every time I hear about the rising cost of healthcare or the downturn of the economy, I can't help but wonder if we'll see relief anytime soon.

Like you, I don't want to hear about businesses leaving my state because of increasing liability expenses, or that a doctor is calling it quits because of the rising cost of malpractice insurance. When I shop for car insurance, I want to pay a reasonable price and not the equivalent of two months' pay.

I am a lot like you—except I'm also a trial lawyer. I represent people from all walks of life who have been injured or killed by another person's carelessness or a defective product. I am a consumer advocate fighting for people who, while minding their own business, were hurt, maimed, or killed by someone else doing something stupid, or as we say in court, "acting negligently." The people I represent have suffered serious, painful, and sometimes permanent injuries or their families have lost a loved one. I pursue the responsible party or corporation to get fair and adequate monetary compensation for my clients.

In our society, money is the only justice an injured person or the family of a wrongfully killed person can get. To be clear, no amount of money will ever bring back a loved one or make up for the debilitating injuries my clients have suffered. Sometimes the money is for lost wages, medical bills, ongoing medical care, and payments for pain and suffering. More importantly, however, the money has a symbolic value. It means that my client's pleas for justice have been heard.

Most of my clients can't afford to pay me by the hour. I am paid through the "poor man's key to the courthouse," the contingency fee. The contingency fee guarantees access to the courthouse for everyone, not just the wealthy or large corporations. If I don't recover a dime on a case, I don't get paid. It's a risk I take. Together with a staff of only a few, I take on multibillion dollar corporations for my clients.

I can only do this because we have something unique and precious in the United States—the civil jury system.

Reza Torkzadeh

INTRODUCTION

Every year in the United States, over 60,000 people are killed and more than 4 million injured in accidents. Types of accidents include those involving motor vehicles, mass transit (e.g., buses, subways, heavy-rail vehicles, light-rail vehicles, electric trolleys, cable cars, and trains), large trucks, motorcycles, pedestrians, boats and personal watercraft, "slip and falls," "trip and falls," elevators and escalators, dog bites and attacks, defective products, medical malpractice, and more.

Today, medical malpractice is the 3rd leading cause of death in America.

Many of these accidents occur because someone else was careless ("negligent," in legalese) and could have prevented the injury or death. When an injury or death is due to the negligent act of another person, the injured victim (or the victim's survivors) may have the right to sue the wrongdoer for monetary damages in a personal injury or wrongful death lawsuit.

The persons injured or killed in these accidents include the operators and passengers of motor vehicles, motorcycles, boats, buses, trains, and subways, and pedestrians, bicyclists, shoppers, product consumers and users, medical patients, and others. Many, if not most, of the injuries and deaths are due to the carelessness of another person, whether it's the driver of the car the victim is riding in, or the driver of another vehicle, but they can also be attributed to defectively designed roads, hazardous railroad crossings, poorly designed or manufactured vehicles, etc. The injuries can range from simple cuts and lacerations to "soft tissue" to damage in the neck, back, and shoulders (whiplash), severe spinal cord injuries resulting in quadriplegia or paraplegia, traumatic brain injury, amputation, life-threatening burns, severe disfigurement, and even death.

If you were injured or have lost a loved one as a result of another person's negligence, this book contains almost everything you will need to know about the personal injury and wrongful death system. It will explain your rights and discuss issues such as how the victim's lawyer's fees are calculated (traditionally through a "contingency fee"), whose fault the accident was, what happens if the injury was partly due to the victim's own carelessness, and how a monetary value is placed on the injury or death.

It will also discuss how a personal injury or wrongful death case proceeds through the legal system, from the moment the person is injured or killed until he (or his survivors) receives a settlement check or a jury delivers a verdict in the victim's favor.

This book is designed to serve as a companion to your lawyer's advice as you pursue a case for personal injuries or wrongful death. It explains things that your attorney may not have time to explain in detail or fail to explain clearly and in terms the ordinary person would understand. Attorneys are busy and may not have the time to give you the clear and thorough explanation that you desire and deserve.

It is our goal and sincere desire to provide you with a sober, practical guide that will help you understand how the California system of personal injury and wrongful death works. We welcome your comments and suggestions regarding how useful you find this information and what other topics we should include in future editions. Please contact us at www.pigeon-lakepublishing.com.

A NOTE ON NEGLIGENCE
AND TORT LAW

Here is some basic information to give you a framework for understanding personal injury and wrongful death cases. There are two broad types of law: criminal law and civil law. Laws relating to personal injury and wrongful death are forms of civil law. In criminal law, the goal of the system is to punish a wrongdoer for committing an act that is offensive to the proper and ordered nature of society. Murder, burglary, arson, and robbery are just a few types of crimes that are recognized as criminal offenses. A person who is convicted of a crime or pleads guilty is punished, whether by a term in jail or prison, a fine, community service, restitution to the wronged person, or a combination of all or some of these. Death by lethal injection is the most severe punishment for a crime, and it is permissible only in certain murder cases that have special circumstances.

Civil law encompasses a wide variety of areas such as bankruptcy, corporate law, wills, trusts and estate planning, family law, probate, worker's compensation, education law, business law, employment law, and that with which we will be concerned: personal injury and wrongful death law, also referred to as "tort" law. "Tort" is a French word meaning "wrong," and that's what a tort is: a civil wrong in which another person is injured or killed or his property is damaged. In civil law, rather than making a wrongdoer serve a sentence in jail or prison, he is ordered to pay the party who suffered the injuries an amount of money designed to make that person "whole" again. Of course, making the person whole again is not always possible, but a monetary award is the only way we know how to compensate the innocent victim.

For example, let's say that a person has had her left arm amputated in an automobile accident caused by another person (the "defendant"). Unfortunately, medical science has not advanced to the point where the severed limb can be re-attached and function good as new. Therefore, the law requires that the defendant pay the injured victim a reasonable sum of money to compensate for her loss.

The most often-used theory of liability in a tort (personal injury) case is what lawyers refer to as "negligence." Probably the best plain English definition of "negligence" is carelessness. For instance, a driver may not be paying attention and therefore fail to see the taillights of the car in front of him as it comes to an abrupt stop, resulting in a rear-end collision; the inattentive driver would be guilty of the tort of negligence.

Perhaps an introductory lesson in law is appropriate here. Negligence is comprised of four parts: (1) the person was required to exercise a minimum amount of due care (safety) to avoid hurting others or causing an accident; (2) the person breached that standard of care by not acting safely (with the "requisite due care"); (3) the person's breach of the standard of care was a "proximate cause" of the incident; and (4) someone else was injured because of the person's negligence (or carelessness).

We are required to exercise sufficient due care at all times so that we do not subject others to an unreasonable risk of harm that may result in their injury or death. When we deviate from the standard of due care and that deviation results in injury to another person or damage to his property, then we are liable for all of the monetary damages to that person that arise out of our careless conduct.

PART I:
WHOSE FAULT IS IT?

1 DETERMINING RESPONSIBILITY

A critical part of a successful personal injury case is proving the fault of the other person. Some cases of responsibility ("liability") for an accident are pretty clear. For instance, if you have been rear-ended in a traffic collision, 99.99 percent of the time it is the fault of the driver who hit you.

In many cases, it is necessary to bring in an expert witness to establish that the other party was at fault. In a traffic accident case, for example, an "accident reconstructionist" may be necessary to prove the fault of the other driver. In a medical malpractice case, a doctor familiar with the procedure and standard of care in the area is vital to proving your case. In a defective product case, engineers or metallurgists may be among the experts called to testify that the product was improperly designed or manufactured, making the product dangerous.

To win in a personal injury case, you must prove that the other person is responsible for your injuries. The standard of care that is used in civil cases such as personal injury is a "preponderance of the evidence"—you must prove that it is more likely than not that the other party was at fault and caused your injuries. This standard of proof is quite a bit lower than that required in criminal cases, where the District Attorney must prove the guilt of the accused beyond a reasonable doubt.

2 WHAT IF BOTH OF YOU WERE AT FAULT?

What happens if you were partly to blame for the accident and are seriously injured? Does this mean that you can't recover a dime from the other party? In the old days, the doctrine of "contributory negligence" applied to bar you from suing the other party, even if you were only one percent at fault! California now uses the "comparative negligence" rule, in which your percent of fault is compared to the other party's percent of fault, and your damages are decreased accordingly.

California uses what is called the "pure" form of the comparative fault doctrine, which allows you to recover your percent of the damages regardless of the percentage of your fault. So if you were, say, 50 percent at fault for the accident, you can recover only 50 percent of the cost of your injuries, lost wages, pain and suffering, and other injuries and damages from the other party. If you were one-third at fault, then you would be entitled to receive only two-thirds of your damages and property damage from the other party. On the other hand, you would be liable for one-third of the other party's personal injuries and property damage.

Let's use as an example a lawsuit arising from the collision between a motor vehicle and a bicycle where the vehicle driver was primarily to blame ("at fault") for the incident. The driver is nevertheless entitled to bring up any fault on the part of the bicyclist to reduce or nullify the bicyclist's right to recover completely. For instance, say that the bicyclist had been riding on the wrong side of the road and the driver, entering the road via a right turn from an intersection or driveway, did not see the bicyclist approaching; the driver may assert the bicyclist's act of riding on the wrong side of the road as a complete or partial bar to the bicyclist's recovery.

The doctrine of comparative fault reduces the amount of money ("damages") the injured bicyclist is entitled to recover. So if a jury determined that the bicyclist's riding the wrong way was 50 percent at fault for the injuries, then the bicyclist's damages are cut in half. In fact, where the bicyclist was riding on the wrong side of the road, a jury may well determine that he was the prime or sole cause of the accident, in which case the motorist might be relieved from all liability for the accident. However, a driver making a right turn onto a road from an intersection or driveway generally has a duty to look both ways before proceeding onto the road to make sure there are no pedestrians or others who might cross his path. Other factors that could be used to reduce or defeat the bicyclist's recovery are: (1) the bicyclist's failure to wear a helmet; (2) failure to have lights on the front and rear of the bicycle; or (3) not wearing a reflective vest while bike riding at night.

PART II:
HOW MUCH IS
MY CASE WORTH?

3 DAMAGES RECOVERABLE IN A PERSONAL INJURY CASE

If you have been injured due to the carelessness of another, the negligent party is responsible for paying all necessary and reasonable medical costs associated with the injury or injuries. Examples could include: (1) the cost of an ambulance to transport you to the hospital; (2) doctors' and hospital expenses; and (3) the costs of all other medical services. The negligent party is also legally responsible for all of your future medical costs attributable to the accident. Additionally, if you need a wheelchair or a full- or part-time attendant, the negligent party must also pay for these.

You are also entitled to recover monetary damages for all of your lost wages past, present, and future. If you are permanently disabled from working as a result of the accident, the amount of your lost wages will be determined by what you would have expected to earn had you not been injured, including raises, bonuses, and promotions. That amount, however, will be reduced ("discounted") to its current value. This means that the amount you would have earned during your lifetime will be reduced to a lump sum that, if invested, would yield how much you would have earned over the next 10, 20, or however many years you would have expected to go on working. If you are permanently injured but are still able to work, although not at your old job and not for the same amount of money you were earning, you are entitled to recover the difference between what you would have made and what you are actually making, the difference being your loss of earning power.

In addition to all medical-related costs and lost earnings, you are entitled to be compensated for pain and suffering arising from the accident, as well as all psychological injuries you suffered as a result of the accident, which often must be supported by the testimony of a psychologist or psychiatrist.

There are two types of damages that can be recovered: economic and non-economic damages. Economic damages include such things as: (1) past, present, and future medical expenses (bills from emergency rooms, hospitals, doctors, physical therapists, rehabilitation therapists, prosthetist, prostheses, wheelchairs, special beds, personal attendants, etc.), and (2) the amount of lost wages or lost earning power, whether the victim will be able to return to work or will have to be retrained for a different profession or occupation, or will be permanently unable to work.

The so-called "non-economic" losses for which you can recover monetary damages include: (1) the intensity and duration of your pain and suffering, (2) emotional distress and mental anguish, (3) physical impairment, (4) grief (but not in wrongful death cases), (5) anxiety, (6) humiliation, (7) inconvenience, (8) fear, anger, and worry, (9) disfigurement, and (10) the "loss of enjoyment of life." Loss of enjoyment of life covers things you used to be able to do but are no longer capable of doing. For instance, if a right-handed father has his right arm amputated and is no longer able to play catch with his son, this is considered part of his loss of enjoyment of life and he deserves to be compensated.

The amount of damages should not only compensate you for damages and injuries you have already suffered, but include compensation for future medical expenses, pain and suffering, new prostheses, complications, etc. Also considered in the amount of your monetary recovery are whether you were in any way responsible for the accident or your injuries ("comparative negligence"), and the amount of insurance and assets the party at fault has.

4 DAMAGES RECOVERABLE IN A WRONGFUL DEATH CASE

When someone is killed because of another person's careless-ness (negligence) or deliberate misconduct, this is called a "wrongful death." For instance, if a person is killed in an auto-mobile accident caused by another motorist who ignored a stop sign, we call that a wrongful death since the death was caused by another person's carelessness.

WHO CAN SUE FOR THE WRONGFUL DEATH OF ANOTHER?

The wrongful death of a person often affects many other people: a spouse, children, grandchildren, employers, friends, and so forth, but only certain persons are entitled to sue the wrongdoer for specified damages. If a 35-year-old married man with three children is killed in an automobile accident caused by another driver's negligence, the spouse (widow) and his three children (the survivors) can all sue the negligent driver. If the man was supporting someone else, such as his elderly parents or a minor under 18, they can also sue to recover their monetary losses, i.e., the money they reasonably could have expected to receive from the deceased person had he not been killed.

WHAT TYPES OF DAMAGES CAN
THE SURVIVORS SUE FOR?

In a wrongful death jury trial in California, it is the jury who will ultimately decide how much money will reasonably compensate the survivor for the loss of the decedent. This compensation is called "damages."

The monetary damages that the jury may award the survivors in a successful wrongful death lawsuit are those that "under all the circumstances of the case, may be just." The survivors are entitled to sue for any and all medical expenses that may have been incurred in attempting to save the victim's life, if such damages have not been recovered in a "survival action." The survivors are also entitled to sue for the lost wages and earnings that the decedent would have contributed to the household during his working years, taking into account raises, bonuses, promotions, and any other types of compensation he would have received from his employer.

Suppose that instead of a 35-year-old working man, the person who was killed was the stay-at-home wife/mother. Since she wasn't working at a paying job, can the survivors seek compensation for "lost earnings?" In the case of a non-working spouse who stays at home and takes care of the children and house, the surviving spouse and children are entitled to receive full and adequate compensation for the loss of services the decedent would have contributed to the household. Studies show that it would cost in the area of $100,000 to hire persons to take the full place of the deceased parent or spouse. For example, who would make the family's meals, get the children ready for school, go shopping for groceries and clothes, do the laundry, prepare the meals, take the kids to dance rehearsals or Boy Scout meetings, etc.?

Although each heir's loss will be different from the others, only one wrongful death lawsuit may be filed. The heir filing the lawsuit must include all of the other heirs entitled to a share of the estate. For instance, if a woman died leaving a husband and three children, if one of the children files a wrongful death action, she must list the decedent's husband and other two children as claimants ("plaintiffs") as well.

One issue with wrongful death cases involving more than one plaintiff is the division of the settlement or award. The jury (or judge, if the trial is by court) must compute the damages by considering the pecuniary loss suffered to all of the heirs and return a verdict for one lump sum. It is then up to the judge to divide the total amount of damages among the individual plaintiffs.

In making her determination as to how much to award each individual plaintiff, the judge will consider such things as the closeness of decedent and the heir, the nature of their relationship, how long they had known each other, the amount of support the decedent was providing for the heir, and other factors.

Evidence that the decedent was unhappy in his marriage and told others that he planned on getting a divorce from his wife does not defeat the wife's claim for damages resulting from her husband's death if no legal action had been taken by the deceased husband, such as obtaining a legal separation or filing for divorce, as couples frequently have disagreements or hard times that make them reassess whether it is worth staying in their marriage. Indeed, even the most happily married couples occasionally have spats in which one threatens to get a divorce. While evidence of a statement that a married person did not get along with his spouse and was going to get a divorce does not bar the other spouse from receiving a share of the wrongful death settlement or award, it may reduce the surviving spouse's share if it bears on the nature and closeness of their relationship.

In California, if a wrongful death case involving multiple plaintiffs is settled out of court and the parties are unable to agree among themselves as to the division of the award, they will have to file an action in court and have a hearing before a judge who will make the ultimate determination as to the settlement's allocation among the heirs. Alternatively, the heirs may agree to have the issue of the division of the settlement proceeds settled out of courts, such as by binding arbitration.

Among the damages recoverable in a wrongful death action in California are economic damages and non-economic damages.

Economic Damages in a Wrongful Death Action:

- Financial support that the decedent would have contributed to the family during the life expectancy of the decedent
- The loss of gifts or benefits
- Funeral and burial expenses
- Reasonable value of household services

Non-Economic Damages in a Wrongful Death Action:

- Loss of love, companionship, comfort, care, assistance, protection, affection, society, and moral support
- Loss of enjoyment of sexual relations (if applicable)
- Loss of training and guidance

The following cannot be considered by a jury when determining loss:

- Grief, sorrow, or mental anguish
- Pain and suffering
- Poverty or wealth of the plaintiff

SURVIVAL ACTIONS

In California, a survival cause of action can be filed by the estate's personal representative or the decedent's successor-in-interest. A survival cause of action can only be brought if the decedent did not immediately die from his or her injuries. A wrongful death survival action may be appropriate even if the deceased lived for a short time after the incident.

Damages recoverable under the statute include "the loss or damage that the decedent sustained or incurred before death, including any penalties or punitive or exemplary damages that the decedent would have been entitled to recover had the decedent lived, and do not include damages for pain, suffering, or disfigurement."

Essentially, the survival statute allows one to "step into the shoes" of the deceased and recover the damages the deceased person would have been entitled to had they lived, including medical expenses and lost wages, as well as penalties or punitive or exemplary damages. One cannot recover damages for pain, suffering, or disfigurement in a survival action.

5 HOW LAWYERS DETERMINE VALUE OF YOUR CASE

Unfortunately, there is no Kelley Blue Book website for lawyers where they can punch in the vital information of your case and the extent of your injuries and it will spit out the exact value. Each case is different. One case may be worth $250,000 while a similar case may be worth only $175,000. It is impossible to list all of the factors that go into deciding how much your case is worth. These factors can include:

- Past and future medical expenses
- Permanency of injury
- Lost wages or disability
- Loss of earning power
- Pain and suffering
- Loss of enjoyment of life
- Chronic pain
- Psychological trauma
- Property damage
- Which part of the state you were injured in (Some regions

are known for their generous verdicts while others are known for their stinginess.)

- Who the injured party is (Cute kids generally bring in a much higher award than the average adult.)

- The makeup of the individual jury

- The appearance, confidence, credentials, and believability of your witnesses as compared to those of the defendant

- How you come across to the jury during your testimony

- Last but not least, the appearance, presentation and competency of your attorney

One case can result in a jury's verdict of $2 million, while a substantially similar case tried in front of another jury in a different part of the state may bring in only $500,000—or even a defense verdict! In fact, two cases involving basically the same set of circumstances may result in drastically different awards, even if they were tried in the same courthouse but before different judges and juries.

Lawyers subscribe to services that tell them how much similar cases are settling for or how much juries are awarding in like cases. However, when it comes down to it, this all depends on the variables of: (1) how sympathetic your client comes across, (2) who the defendant is and how evil she looks, and (3) how clear liability is. The clearer the liability, the more willing the jury is to put a higher amount on the injuries and damages you suffered.

PART III:
BEFORE YOU SPEAK
TO A LAWYER

Hiring a lawyer and starting any kind of legal action can often be a complicated process. A personal injury claim is no different and the most important decision you will make is hiring the right lawyer to represent you and your family. It is up to you to arm your lawyer with any and all information that you have to help them effectively represent you.

There are a few things your personal injury lawyer will ask you at your initial consultation. Knowing the answers ahead of time will help out in the long run.

WHO, WHAT, WHEN WHERE, WHY AND HOW

1. Who was involved?

When your accident happened, who else was there besides you? If it was a car accident, were you carrying passengers? What were their names? If there was another party involved in the accident, what was their name? Were there any other people with the at-fault party? If your accident happened on someone else's property, whose property was it? What is their relationship to you? Were these your friends? Neighbors? Employers? Children? Relatives?

Knowing the names and relationships of everyone involved right off the bat will speed up the entire intake process. These are the first questions your lawyer will ask you, and they set the tone of the rest of their investigation of the incident. The last thing you want is to be really deep into the case when your lawyer suddenly gets a phone call from another injured party they didn't even know was involved or a witness who saw the entire incident.

2. Who are the witnesses?

Again, this is a time where you need to be able to say not just who those involved are, but who are they in relation to you. Is the witness related to you? A friend? A random passer-by on the street? Were they a co-worker or a supervisor?

Knowing who they are, but also who they are to you, goes a long way for your lawyer in trying to establish the credibility of your witnesses. A family member who was in your car at the time of an accident may not be as credible as a totally independent witness with no interest on either side.

Witnesses very much need to be independent. Having a neutral, third-party account of any kind of accident can be vital to proving your case. If you can tell your lawyer up front, "This person saw the whole thing, this is who they are, this is what they know, and this is their relationship to me," the investigation into your case can be sped up substantially.

It's also important to have full names and contact information for these witnesses, since your lawyer will need to speak with them. If you don't have this information and it will be your lawyer's responsibility to track down witnesses and take these statements. There are many ways an effective attorney can track down witnesses.

3. Who were the First Responders?

When your accident happened, did the police respond? Were there paramedics or firefighters? Was there a doctor who just so happened to be there and administered first aid? If the accident was in a public place, did the facility have security personnel that responded?

You also need to have the documentation of this response or tell your attorney so that they can obtain any report. First responder reports such as a police report, paramedic report, or incident report on a premises liability case can be critical in any case. You can never really have too much documentation when it comes to an accident, and these reports are some of the most important things to have at the out-set or early on in any case.

In the case of a good Samaritan who happened to be in the right place at the right time and assisted you—you'll need their information also. When it comes to a good Samaritan, there's a number of implications that your lawyer will need to investigate. If they administered any kind of first aid or medical attention, your lawyer needs to speak to them about it. If they attempted to repair something, or spoke to police on your behalf, this is important. Make sure you have this person's name and correct contact information before your consultation.

4. What exactly happened?

Having this prepared might be the most important thing of all. You need to be able to tell your lawyer a detailed account of everything that happened, as you remember it, to the best of your abilities. This is your account of the accident and might very well be the foundation upon which the entire case is built. It's important to have this prepared and prepared correctly.

Your lawyer will ask you about many of the details, so you'll want to make special note of everything that happened and everything that was around you at the time of the accident. Again, this is "to the best of your ability." A lawyer will ask for some details you think are unimportant, but might dictate the entire direction of your case. Know these details.

The timeline of your accident is important as well. In what order did everything happen, and when did it happen? Things like time of day, chronology of events, change of location, incidents leading up to and following the accident, and other key elements are all vital to your case. If this is at all foggy to you, it might help to go back over some of the documentation to jog your memory.

Many people have a tendency to bend a story a bit, to make

themselves look better and the other party at fault. Lawyers hear this all the time, and it is the tall grass they must wade through to find the truth. There is no need to inject opinion or judgement into your account of the accident at this point. Stick to just the important facts of what happened, where it happened, when it happened, and in what order it happened. Leave your opinions of the other party or your assessment of fault out of it.

Remember, accident cases are built on many things, but details are one of the biggest. You want to give every detail you can, and let your lawyer focus on what's important. What you think is trivial might end up to be the most important thing of all.

5. What were you doing?

This is kind of an aside from your fact-based account of the accident, but it's important enough that it gets its own question.

You'll want to be able to say what you were doing in the time leading up and following to the accident. If you were in a car, where were you going? If you were in a public place, what were you doing there? If you were at work, what was the task in front of you? Where were you coming from when you got to the scene of the accident? Where did you go afterwards? What was going on around you right before the accident happened?

Make sure these details are clear not only for you, but for your witnesses and, if possible, the other party or parties.

Sometimes people's memories of an accident can be hazy or even incomplete. This is okay. There's no reason to reject large chunks of an accident account just because your memory is touch-and-go. The rule-of-thumb is that it's okay if you don't remember everything exactly, but always tell your lawyer what you remember and always tell the truth.

6. When did it happen?

Separate from the timeline of the accident, the "when" of your accident is immensely important to the case. This means knowing time of day, date, and when applicable, the year.

Knowing the exact time of an accident can go a long way in proving a wide variety of things. Was the sun in someone's eyes? Was there a normal or high amount of traffic at the time? Had a sporting event just let out? Was it a weekend or a weekday? What was the weather that day? How much time has passed between your injury and now? Has there been a normal amount of healing time?

If you don't remember an exact time or date, refer to the police or incident report.

7. Where did it happen?

This is another area where specificity is important. What street where you on? What part of the public area were you in? What floor were you on? What lane were you in? Were you entering or exiting an intersection? Were you on your way up the stairs or down? You will need to know exactly where everything happened, with as much detail as possible.

If this was on a street, know the street name and the number of the block. Also, record as many cross-streets as possible, and the "block north of/block south of" information. Landmarks that were near you at the time are also of the utmost importance.

In addition to the location of the accident, you'll also want to know where you were going and where you were coming from. What route were you taking? Did you cut through a cafeteria to get to the elevator? Were you taking a side entrance or exit? Were you driving a shortcut to your destination? What was your final destination? Where did you start from? What was your route?

Exact location of the incident is very important. This helps your lawyer build a "model" of the accident. It places you in a specific place and time for the narrative they are creating for your case. It allows your lawyer to build the events with enough detail that it accounts for any variables or deviation.

Again, if your memory is not exactly perfect, this is okay. Try your best to fill in the gaps by reading the first responder's reports or if you can, going back to the scene of the accident. If you return to the scene, you are recording these details of location in a better frame of mind and with the intention of recording things accurately. This is not a time for you to do accident investigation, however. Simply record the names of streets and landmarks for your account of the story. Do not try to piece together the events or look for new information.

8. How did the accident happen?

This is a little bit different from the "what happened" description. Your lawyer is going to want a more technical account of the accident. This is the time for nuts-and-bolts descriptions of the accident.

You'll need to know very specific things like the speed a car was driving. How fast a crowd was walking. If a door opened inwards or outwards. Which way a steering wheel was pointed. Other details like sounds, sights, and even smells will be of the utmost importance.

A lawsuit like this is an exercise in details. When your lawyer is proving your case, they are going to delve into the nitty-gritty of everything that happened. When you can give a second, more in-depth account of your story, this gives your lawyer plenty to work with.

9. Why do you think the accident happened?

Finally, after everything else, the last part is when you get to use your opinion. Every other question is a "just the facts" situation, but this is when you get to express your opinion.

Was the other party not paying attention? Was there defective equipment involved? Did someone appear to be intoxicated? Was someone in charge not paying attention? Was the other party acting recklessly? Was something just not right with the situation?

You were there, and your lawyer was not. Once you've given all the facts, all the figures, all the details, your opinion will help immensely. This is an eyewitness interpretation that only you can give. This is only useful if you have already supplied your lawyer with the strict details. If you start with your opinion, that's just going to complicate things.

Another reason your lawyer will want to hear your opinion and interpretation is to see if there are details missing. If your answer to many of these questions ends up being "I don't know," there might be something else going on, like a brain injury. Should there be large gaps in your account and interpretation of the accident, you and your lawyer might want to look at some further medical investigations.

WHAT IS IT YOU ARE TRYING TO ACCOMPLISH?

When you seek legal counsel after an accident, you do so with a goal in mind. Whether that goal is financial in nature or based in principle, you have a goal. Knowing what your ultimate goal is will help your lawyer plan your case correctly. If you are looking to achieve ABC, you need to tell your lawyer that so they don't put together a plan to get you WXYZ. More than likely, in your initial consultation, your lawyer will ask you in no uncertain terms, "What is it you'd like to accomplish?"

Know this ahead of time, but more importantly, be honest. If you are looking for money to see a doctor, tell your lawyer. If you are trying to take care of some of the mounting medical bills, tell your lawyer. This could dictate the entire direction of your case and could even be a make it or break it kind of question.

Too often, clients will come into an initial consultation and tell the lawyer, "I want justice," and nothing else. While this is a perfectly reasonable answer, it doesn't tell your lawyer a whole lot. What "justice" looks like to you might be different from what it looks like to someone else. Of course you want justice, but you'll want to know what justice is before you ask for it.

In wrongful death cases, many clients are looking to hold the responsible party accountable. This is also perfectly reasonable. If this is your answer to the question, say it. There's nothing wrong with wanting to hold someone accountable when you've lost a loved one. It's not a bad thing, it's just something your lawyer needs to know.

Knowing your ultimate goal is possibly one of the most important things to your case other than the accounts of the accident.

WHAT ARE YOUR DAMAGES?

If you're seeking legal counsel for an injury, you're dealing with damages of some kind. Your life has been negatively impacted by the aftermath of this accident and you're having to clean up the mess made by someone else's negligence. Before you can recover any of these damages, your lawyer needs to know what they are.

1. Financial Damages

Have you had to pay for something because of this accident? Are there medical bills you've had to pay? Did you lose property? All of these things amount to financial damages and you'll need record of them.

If you have some records of bills or expenses you've had to pay, or that you currently owe because of the accident, make sure to send your lawyer copies.

As a victim of an accident, the burden of proof is on you, the

Plaintiff, to prove your harms and damages. That's why it's so important to have proof of all the expenses that you've paid or you owe to prove your economic damages.

Economic damages can include loss of earnings, so make sure you accurately record how much time you missed from work and how much income that translates into. This can be easily done by looking at paycheck stubs and bank account statements.

2. Quality Of Life

An accident can not only disrupt your life temporarily, but there are times that an accident can have catastrophic impact permanently—not only on your life, but on your entire family.

You might not be able to work, enjoy hobbies, spend time with family like you used to, or even function properly. These are damages as well, and the law says that you are entitled to be compensated for them.

When you speak or meet with your lawyer, you'll want to know the answer to some of these question: How has the accident affected your life? What are you not able to do that you did before? What are you struggling with? How have you changed and how has the accident left you?

Think about your everyday life. Has this accident made it difficult for you to do everyday things like brushing your teeth, cooking meals, or driving a car? Have you had injuries that affected your sleep cycle? Are you having trouble hearing or speaking? Are you having trouble concentrating or problems with your memory?

You also want to be clear about the psychological damages you've incurred. Have you had nightmares? Are you afraid to go back to certain places or to drive again? Are you having anxiety? Know these things before you go in and do not be afraid to discuss them.

We call these damages "the intangibles." They are things you cannot quantify or put an exact dollar amount on. This is where you and your lawyer must work together very closely so that they truly understand every aspect of your life that has been affected.

While you cannot show a dollar amount for the damage to your overall quality of life, you'll want to tell your lawyer about it in detail, without holding back any information. Make sure that your lawyer truly understands how your life has been affected.

PART IV
WORKING WITH YOUR ATTORNEY

6 FINDING THE RIGHT ATTORNEY

Finding the right lawyer to handle your case can be a challenge. Being in a serious accident or having to deal with the death of a loved one is a traumatic and life-changing event. Choosing the right lawyer is one of the most important decisions that you can make on your path to recovery.

In serious injury and wrongful death cases, it is vital that you speak to a qualified personal injury lawyer as soon as possible. Witness statements should be taken by the lawyer or his or her associates and potential evidence needs to be preserved. Photographs of the scene of the incident and inspections of any products or machinery that was defective or malfunctioned need to be taken before changes occur or repairs are made. Your lawyer may want to have an expert in the field, such as a traffic accident reconstructionist or metallurgist, visit the scene of the accident or inspect the product and gather evidence in your favor.

An experienced personal injury lawyer or law firm will know the type of investigation and fact finding that needs to be done in your particular case. The longer you wait to retain a personal injury lawyer, the worse it will be for you. Witnesses may move out of the area, the product that injured you may be destroyed or repaired, and the company of the employee that hurt you may go out of business.

In California there are more than 160,000 active lawyers. While the State Bar of California provides certification in some specialized areas of law—such as family law, taxation, and criminal law—it does not provide specialization certificates in the area of personal injury and wrongful death law. However, if you have been seriously injured or had a loved one killed in an accident, you will want to focus your search for an attorney in the area of personal injury lawyers.

There are many places you can begin your search for an experienced personal injury lawyer. With just a few keystrokes, the Internet will pull hundreds of lawyers for you in seconds. Whether you are blindly searching the Internet or researching a lawyer or law firm that was recommended to you by a friend, it is important to choose a lawyer that you are comfortable with.

It is always a good idea to meet and speak with more than one lawyer before making your final decision on which lawyer to hire. You should make a list of questions to ask the lawyer prior to meeting with him or her in order to help in your determination if this is the right lawyer for you. Decide what matters the most to you and what you hope to achieve, and make a list of what to discuss with the lawyer.

Here are some suggested questions to get you started:

- Have you handled this type of case before and what was the result?

- What should I expect throughout the legal process?

- How involved will I be in the case?

- Will you keep me regularly informed of the progress of the case?

- Will you be handling my case personally or will others in the law firm be handling much of the case?

- Do you feel comfortable representing me?

Make sure that the law firm understands your objectives and goals, and knows what it means to be in your shoes. It is of the utmost importance that the lawyer representing you can effectively convey your message and your struggles to others. Whether it is to an insurance adjuster who will attempt to make a settlement or a jury that will make a monetary award, it is critical that your lawyer knows exactly how your life has been changed by the accident and can effectively communicate that to the insurance adjuster or a jury.

7 THE CONTINGENCY FEE AGREEMENT

Accident cases involving personal injury or wrongful death are usually taken on a "contingency fee" basis in the United States. This means that your lawyer gets paid only if she is successful in getting a settlement or jury award for you. Some lawyers use a hybrid form of fees in which they ask for a certain non-refundable fee up front, such as $2,500, and then take their full percentage of the fee after the case has settled or a jury has awarded you a specific sum. Sometimes an attorney will ask the client to pay for costs and expenses as they are incurred, rather than waiting until the end of the case. This is especially true of newer lawyers or lawyers who do not have much confidence in your case and don't want to put up a couple of thousand dollars getting expert witnesses to testify on your behalf.

In personal injury cases, the amount of the lawyer's fees generally ranges from 25 to 50 percent of the gross settlement or jury award. Some lawyers have a standard 33 or 40 percent of the gross settlement or award regardless of when the case settles. Other lawyers have fees that increase as certain landmarks are passed. For instance, an attorney may charge 25 percent if the case settles before a complaint (the formal document filed in court to start a lawsuit) is filed, 33 to 40 percent after the complaint is filed but before a trial date is assigned, and 40 to 50 percent after the trial date is assigned. Some lawyers are now charging 50 percent of the gross settlement or award, regardless of when the case settles (e.g., before a complaint is filed).

Note that the lawyer's fee normally comes out of the gross settlement or jury award, before any other costs are deducted. Costs and expenses that come out of your share after the lawyer has been paid can include:

- An expert in traffic accident reconstruction
- Medical doctors testifying to the extent and permanency of your injuries
- Rehabilitation experts
- Physical therapists
- Court reporter's costs
- Court costs and expenses

You should try to negotiate with the lawyer for her contingent fee to be based on the net recovery, after costs and expenses have been deducted.

PART V:
HOW A CASE PROCEEDS THROUGH THE JUSTICE SYSTEM

8 BEFORE FILING A LAWSUIT

The first step in a claim that will wend its way through the legal system is, of course, an injury or the death of one or more persons due to the fault of another person or persons. Part VI of this book discusses some of the more common causes of personal injury and wrongful death, while Part VII addresses some of the more common injuries encountered.

If your claim involves a public entity (a governmental agency), be it a city, county, the State of California, or the United States, you must act quickly. Claims must be made with the appropriate governmental agency within a certain time limit, usually six months (although, in some cases, it can be considerably less).

The first focus of a claim is ensuring that the injured victim has received or is receiving the proper medical care. An experienced personal injury law firm usually knows which doctors are considered the "tops" in their field and they can refer you to those doctors as appropriate.

As soon as you have retained (formally hired) the law firm or attorney, they will begin an immediate investigation into the cause(s) of the accident. In an automobile accident case, an investigation may include:

- Sending an investigator to the scene of the accident to

take pictures of the accident site at approximately the same time of day as the accident occurred

- Taking pictures of the cars before they are repaired to show where and how badly the vehicles were damaged
- Finding witnesses and taking their statements
- Directing you to a good doctor to evaluate how badly injured you are, the type of treatment you will need in the future, etc.

Depending upon the type of accident that you were injured in and the severity of your injuries, various experts may be retained to discover the cause of the accident or to prove the extent and permanence of your injuries. This may involve hiring an accident reconstruction expert, medical doctors, experts in product design and manufacture, psychotherapists, economists, accountants, pain management specialists, etc.

After the initial investigation has been performed, the lawyer will contact the insurance company's adjuster and begin preliminary settlement talks. Insurance company adjusters keep their jobs by settling cases for as little as possible, so it is typical for the insurance adjuster to blame part or all of the accident on you or argue that you are exaggerating your injuries.

As your injuries begin to heal (or if you have suffered paralysis, an amputation, and/or a traumatic brain injury), your attorney will start to calculate the value of your case. As we discussed in Part IV, Working with Your Attorney, your attorney will put a monetary value on your case based on a number of factors. The other driver's insurance company should promptly pay the policy limits if your injuries and resulting disability run into the millions of dollars but all the person who hit you has is an insurance policy for $100,000 and there is no question that the other driver was at fault for the accident.

When the insurance policy is sufficient to pay the damages

or your injuries and lost wages clearly exceed the amount of the policy limits, your lawyer may send a "demand letter" demanding that the insurance company pay the full amount to settle the case and avoid an expensive trial that it is likely to lose. On the insurance company's part, the insurance adjuster may send your lawyer a letter offering to settle the case for a certain amount that is considerably less than the insurance limits. If the two figures are in the same ballpark, further settlement negotiations with the insurance company or their lawyer may prove fruitful. If, however, the two sides have drastically different views on the value of the case, then it will be necessary to resort to the legal system. Over 95 percent of all personal injury and wrongful death cases settle without going to trial—sometimes on the courthouse steps the day the trial is to begin. Also, many cases are settled at mediation or arbitration.

9 TAKING THE CASE TO TRIAL

If you are unable to reach a reasonable settlement with the insurance company, your lawyer will file a "Complaint for Damages" against the party or parties who injured you. The person who hurt you (or her insurance company) will then have to file a formal response (called the "Answer") to the Complaint within a certain time, usually 30 days. If the defendant fails to file an Answer within 30 days, and your lawyer has not granted the defendant an extension of time in which to file, your lawyer may file for a Default Judgment.

After the Complaint and Answer have been filed, the fact-finding part of the lawsuit begins. This is formally known as "discovery." Usually the first step in discovery is sending specific questions ("Written Interrogatories") to the other party (the "defendant"). The defendant must answer the interrogatories under penalty of perjury. After interrogatories have been served and answered, your lawyer will want to take the deposition of the other party. Likewise, the lawyer for the defendant will usually want to take your deposition. A deposition is a formal examination of one party by the other party's attorney.

If you are being deposed, the deposition will most likely take place in the other party's lawyer's office. A court reporter will swear you in just like in "real" court and will take down everything that is said during the deposition (except where the attorneys speak off the record). During the discovery process, the lawyers will also want to take the depositions of any expert witnesses the other lawyer plans on calling at trial, such as an accident reconstructionist or medical expert.

With input from the attorneys for both sides, the judge will set a trial date. Before the date for the trial arrives, the judge will hold a pre-trial settlement conference with the parties and their attorneys in an effort to reach an agreeable settlement. If the parties are unable to agree to settle the case for a certain amount, the case will proceed to trial. It is not all that unusual for the parties to settle the case on the courthouse steps on the morning that the trial is set to begin.

At the trial, you, the injured victim, are referred to as the "plaintiff." As already noted, the person who hurt you is referred to as the "defendant." As the plaintiff seeking compensation from the defendant, you have the burden of proving your case. You are required to prove to a "preponderance of the evidence" that your injuries and damages were caused by the defendant. Preponderance of the evidence means that you must prove that it is more likely than not that you were injured and that the defendant caused your injuries. All you need to do is tip the scales of justice in your favor ever so slightly. Thus, if you can prove that the defendant's wrongful act was 51 percent or greater, you will win the case. Contrast this standard of proof with the criminal standard of proof, in which the District Attorney must prove "beyond a reasonable doubt" that the accused committed the crime. The civil standard of "more likely than not" is considerably lower than the criminal "reasonable doubt" test.

Before the trial begins, a jury must be selected. (In some personal injury and wrongful death cases, the parties will want to have the case heard and decided by the judge rather than a jury, but this is relatively rare in personal injury cases.) A group ("pool") of potential jurors will be brought to the courtroom.

It used to be that 12 jurors heard a civil case and had to bring back a unanimous verdict. Now, in California, only nine of the 12 jurors must agree with the verdict for the plaintiff to prevail.

Some judges prefer to do the bulk of the questioning of each juror themselves to decide whether the potential juror can be fair and impartial in making a decision in the case. Other judges let the lawyers do most of the questioning.

After the jury has been selected and sworn in ("empanelled"), the plaintiff presents his "case-in-chief." Before the trial testimony begins, the judge may briefly tell the jury what the case is all about. The plaintiff's attorney starts the trial with an opening statement. Opening statements are designed for the lawyers to state what facts they intend to prove to the jury. The attorneys may not argue any aspect of the case during opening statements. Arguments, such as what the facts prove or the credibility of a witness, are saved for the end of trial. After the plaintiff's attorney has made an opening statement, the defendant's attorney may wish to make an opening statement for the defense, or he may wait until the plaintiff's case-in-chief is rested.

In the typical personal injury case, the plaintiff testifies under oath as to the facts leading up to and causing the accident, his physical injuries, property damage, pain and suffering, past and future medical expenses, loss of enjoyment of life, etc. The plaintiff's attorney will present the testimony of experts in their various fields—e.g., accident reconstructionists, medical doctors, economists, accountants, and pain management specialists—to prove how the accident happened and why the defendant was as fault, the injuries and surgeries the plaintiff has had and any future surgeries the plaintiff may need to undergo, and how his medical injuries will impact the rest of his life. He will also introduce the testimony of forensic accountants to prove how much loss the plaintiff has had and will have in the future due to a diminished ability to work (or complete disability), and the costs of medical care the plaintiff will need in the future. At the end of each witness's testimony, the defendant has the right to cross-examine the witness and try to discredit or poke holes in the witness's testimony.

Once the plaintiff has finished presenting his case-in-chief, the defendant has the right to present her side of the case. At the close of the plaintiff's case-in-chief, the defendant's lawyer may ask the judge to enter a "nonsuit" against the plaintiff, based on the argument that the plaintiff failed to prove all of the elements of his case or failed to prove that the defendant was in any way responsible for the plaintiff's harm. If the judge grants the defendant's Motion for Nonsuit, the trial is over, the defendant being declared the winner.

If the trial judge denies the Motion for Nonsuit, the defendant presents her side of the case. The defendant may take the witness stand herself or present an accident reconstruction expert witness to contradict the plaintiff's expert's testimony, as well as putting on the stand expert physicians, accountants, and other witnesses in an attempt to prove that the plaintiff's damages are nowhere near what he is asking the jury to award. After the defense counsel rests the defendant's case, the plaintiff has the right to call any witnesses to dispute ("rebut") any or all of the defendant's witnesses.

After both sides have rested their respective cases and all rebuttal witnesses have been called and testified, the judge instructs the jury as to what law(s) to apply. (Before the trial even began, the lawyers for the plaintiff and the defendant will have submitted the jury instructions they would like the judge to read to the jury at the end of the case).

After the judge has read all of the jury instructions to the jury, the jury retires to the jury room for deliberations of the merits of the case. The first order of business for the jury is selecting the foreperson, who will be in charge of keeping the deliberations civil. In many cases, after the foreperson has been selected, the jury will immediately take a vote by private ballot to see how close they are to getting a consensus. Lawyers used to believe that if the jury reached a verdict quickly it was in favor of the defense, while longer deliberations benefited the plaintiff. However, that is just an old wife's tale and nothing can be read into how long it takes for the jury to reach its verdict. As noted above, in civil cases, a unanimous verdict is not required; only nine jurors out of the 12 need agree for the plaintiff to win.

With the exception of plaintiffs in Small Claims Court actions, if you disagree with the verdict or with any of the judge's rulings during the trial, you have the right to appeal it to an intermediate court, the District Court of Appeal (DCA) for your area. A panel of a DCA consists of three judges whose review is limited to facts and exhibits entered into evidence at your trial. If applicable, the DCA will also decide whether a trial judge's decision was wrong regarding not allowing you to present helpful evidence to your case to the jury. The appellate judges read all of the transcripts relating to the trial, whether the testimony was made in open court in front of the jury or in the judge's private chambers with just the judge, lawyers, and court reporter present. The court will not consider any testimony or evidence that you or your attorney forgot to bring up at trial. However, if there is newly discovered evidence since the trial, the DCA may consider it or, if it is important, the DCA may send the case back to the lower court for a retrial in light of the newly discovered evidence.

The DCA also reviews the law applied in the case, to make sure the trial judge did not make an erroneous decision based on a misinterpretation of the law or give an instruction to the jury that misstated the law. If the trial judge's error is considered harmless (i.e., it didn't affect the outcome of the case) the DCA deems such error harmless and affirms the verdict. If, however, the error was "prejudicial," that is, it prevented either side from getting a fair trial, the DCA will call the mistake prejudicial and send the case back ("remand") to the trial judge for a new trial or other reparative action.

If either party is dissatisfied with the DCA's decision, they may try to appeal the case to the California Supreme Court. Unlike DCAs, which must consider and rule on every case appealed to them, the California Supreme Court only takes those cases it wishes to hear.

PART VI:
TYPES AND EXAMPLES OF COMMON ACCIDENTS

10 AUTOMOBILE ACCIDENTS

Automobile accidents are the leading cause of death for Americans under the age of 34. Each year, there are about 6.5 million automobile accidents resulting in nearly 40,000 deaths and 3.5 million injuries. Age is a factor in many auto accidents. Drivers between the ages of 16 and 20 and those over 70 have a much higher percentage of accidents than people in other age ranges.

COMMON CAUSES OF MOTOR VEHICLE ACCIDENTS

The most common type of auto accident is the rear-end collision. For instance, a car stops at a stop sign, a red light, or in rush-hour traffic, and the vehicle behind it crashes into the back of the first car. The errant driver often simply wasn't paying sufficient attention to the road in front of him; by the time he realized that the car in front had stopped, it was too late to avoid an accident. Abruptly reducing your speed to look at the aftermath of an accident ("rubbernecking"), causing the vehicle behind you to crash into your car, is another common cause of rear-end collisions.

If you were stopped at a stop sign or red light when your vehicle got rear-ended, in 99.99 percent of the cases the driver who hit you from behind will be legally responsible; the law requires that you drive a safe distance behind other cars so you won't run into them if you have to stop suddenly. The one major exception to this rule is when a driver suddenly pulls in front of you and brakes hard, causing you to rear-end his vehicle. This type of case is used by criminals to defraud insurance companies out of money, because they know how hard it is to disprove liability in rear-end collisions. They have a network of seedy doctors who treat the "injured victim" until their bill reaches an astronomical amount, and then members of the group, which may be fronted by an unethical lawyer, negotiate with the insurance company for large settlements. This kind of bogus claim drives everybody's insurance premiums up and is more common—and lucrative—than you may think.

The failure of a car turning left at an intersection to yield the right-of-way to oncoming traffic is the second most common cause of traffic accidents. A driver making a left turn must yield the right-of-way to oncoming traffic. The left-turning driver may not be paying attention and may not see an oncoming vehicle. Or she may see the oncoming vehicle but think (erroneously) that she has sufficient time to make a left turn. The driver may misjudge the speed and distance of the oncoming vehicle. The left-turning driver may speed up, thinking that she can make the turn before the other vehicle reaches the intersection. Sometimes the oncoming car is exceeding the posted speed limit by 10, 15, or more miles per hour, making it harder to judge how much time one has to make a safe left turn.

Another leading cause of automobile accidents is driver distraction or inattentiveness; the driver simply isn't paying sufficient attention to the road in front of him, the flow of traffic, and/or the condition of the road. The driver may be distracted by changing the radio station or volume, picking up a dropped object, eating, grooming in the car, talking to passengers, tending to a small child, dealing with a pet, or engaging in a number of other activities that takes his eyes off the road. It only takes a few seconds of not watching the road and the cars in front of you for an accident to happen.

In California, the use of hand-held cell phones is banned when driving. Still, research shows that people who use hands-free cell phones are at a much higher risk of getting into an accident than drivers who don't use cell phones. The problem is that the driver's attention is focused on the telephone conversation she is having, rather than on the road in front of her and the surrounding traffic.

Alcohol is involved in approximately 40 percent of automobile accident cases. The legal limit of blood alcohol content (BAC) for criminal purposes is .08. But a person with a BAC of .05 or .06 (or even lower) may be sufficiently impaired to affect his judgment and reflexes, resulting in a traffic accident. Because automobile injury cases are tried in the civil courts, it is not necessary to prove that the at-fault driver met the criminal definition of impairment to hold him legally responsible ("liable") for the monetary damages incurred by the victim, such as medical expenses, lost wages, and damages for pain and suffering.

Aggressive driving is a frequent cause of automobile accidents. This includes such high-risk activities as tailgating, speeding, excessive lane changing, failing to use signal lights to indicate a turn or a lane change, cutting off other vehicles, failing to yield the right of way, and blatantly ignoring traffic signals or signs.

Failing to maintain one's vehicle in proper operating condition is another frequent cause of traffic accidents. Worn-out brakes are a major cause of many accidents. Tires that do not have enough tread left to stop the car—especially in an emergency—are a common cause of traffic accidents. The risk of getting into a traffic accident in a car with bald tires increases dramatically when there is water on the road, such as with rainfall or icing. Other mechanical causes of an accident may be a tire blowout; a failure of the steering system; axle failure; defects in the door latches, fuel system, airbags, seat belts, or seat backs; and insufficient roof strength to prevent a collapse in the case of a turnover. As you can see, in addition to carelessness on the part of the vehicle's owner, the design or manufacturing of a vehicle may also be defective. This is true of Sport Utility Vehicles (SUVs), which have a high center of gravity and are more likely to roll over in an accident.

Weather conditions can lead to many accidents. Rain, ice, or snow on the asphalt can cause problems with traction and make it take longer to stop a car than if the road surface was dry. Southern California gets a relatively small amount of rain; when it does rain, oil seeps to the surface of the road, increasing the hazard of a slippery surface. Also, since it rains so infrequently in Southern California, drivers have little experience with how to drive safely on slick roads, resulting in a dramatic increase in accidents during rainy periods.

A growing number of automobile accidents in California involve street racing. In some cases, two drivers get into a race, and then a pedestrian or other vehicle starts to cross the road; the speeding street racer may not be able to stop in time to avoid the accident. Or one of the cars could lose control and hit a pole or tree straight-on, causing serious injury or death. In cases of death, the driver of the other vehicle may face serious criminal charges.

Sometimes an accident occurs on the freeway or a highway when someone is driving in the wrong direction and collides head-on with a vehicle coming from the opposite direction. Frequently the wrong-way driver is very drunk or high on drugs and unwittingly got on the wrong traffic ramp. But some of these drivers are intent on committing suicide and have no regard for the lives of the persons in the other vehicle who will be injured or killed in the collision.

Sometimes an auto accident will be due to the negligence of a public entity—the United States, the State of California, a county, or a city—in designing, constructing, or maintaining public roadways. For instance, a public entity may be liable for deaths or injuries related to road construction accidents resulting from its negligence, if the public entity created a dangerous condition with its property for which it had actual or constructive notice that the condition posed a risk of harm to persons using the road. Constructive notice means that the dangerous condition of the roadway had existed long enough that the public entity should have known about it, such as from a previous accident or a complaint.

Single-car accidents can happen for a number of reasons. Perhaps the driver was speeding or driving under the influence of alcohol or drugs, or there may be a defect in the car that caused it to go out of control. Another common cause of single-vehicle accidents is an unsafe and dangerous design of the road. Faulty signage or road painting can cause a traffic accident. Unsafe railroad crossings are responsible for a number of injuries and deaths each year. Single-vehicle accidents can also result from the negligent design of the vehicle, such as with 15-passenger vans and SUVs: both have a higher center of gravity and may roll over while the driver is negotiating a sharp turn.

Suppose a vehicle hits you and causes injuries to you and your passenger but it leaves the scene before you get a chance to exchange information such as name, address, insurance coverage, registered owner, and the like. Cases such as these are treated as uninsured motorist claims. Any recovery for the personal injuries suffered by you and your passengers must be made under the uninsured motorist clause of your own automobile insurance policy. But what if you didn't purchase uninsured motorist coverage to save a few bucks on your policy? Then you are out of luck. If you were in any way at fault for the accident, and you have some assets, such as a house or investment portfolio, your passengers may end up seeking compensation for their medical bills, lost wages, pain and suffering, and other damages from you personally.

Sport Utility Vehicle (SUV) rollover accidents seriously injure or kill about 10,000 people in the United States each year, more than side and rear crashes combined. SUVs and 15-passenger vans are much more likely to roll over or flip over than standard passenger vans and automobiles. Rollover accidents are responsible for 51 percent of all deaths in SUVs, 36 percent of deaths in trucks (mainly pickup trucks), and 19 percent of deaths in passenger automobiles. SUVs were originally designed as off-road vehicles, and their high center of gravity makes them top heavy. An SUV traveling at freeway speeds or above is most likely to rollover when the driver performs a simple driving maneuver, like turning to avoid an object in the road or over-steering when passing another vehicle.

One of the main reasons for this high rate of death and serious bodily harm in rollovers, such as paralysis due to a spinal cord injury or head injuries including traumatic brain injury, is crushed roofs. The more the roof is crushed, the more severe the injuries and the risk of death. The current roof-strength standard is some 35 years old and many serious injuries or deaths could be averted by higher strength standards. A study by the National Highway Traffic Safety Administration (NHTSA) revealed a clear statistical correlation between the amount a roof collapsed into the passenger compartment and the severity of injury. In cases where the vehicle's occupants were not injured, the vehicles averaged 16 centimeters of lost headroom due to roof intrusion. In accidents with the most serious injuries, the vehicles lost an average of 24 centimeters of headroom in the rollover crashes.

USING THE POLICE REPORT TO DETERMINE LIABILITY

Let's suppose that you've been in an automobile accident and a police officer that arrived on the scene prepared an accident report. Is this the ultimate and final say on the cause of the accident? No. Unless the police officer was an eyewitness to the accident, the police report is considered to be "hearsay"—facts based on what the officer heard from others as opposed to seeing it himself—and it is not admissible as evidence in court. Of course, information contained in the police report may be extremely helpful to your attorney, such as the gathered names and statements of witnesses, diagrams of the accident scene, measurements of skid marks, showing where the car was struck, etc.

DOES THE OTHER PERSON HAVE INSURANCE OR SIGNIFICANT ASSETS?

Suppose you were seriously injured in a head-on collision caused by a drunk driver who crossed the double lines separating the directions of traffic. Liability is clear and your damages—financially, medically, and emotionally—run into the hundreds of thousands of dollars. But the problem is that the driver of the other car has no insurance (is an "uninsured motorist") or low insurance policy limits (an "underinsured motorist") and little in the way of possessions that could be sold to pay you. A million dollar judgment isn't worth the paper it's written on if the person doesn't have insurance or significant assets to pay the judgment. We've all heard the axiom hundreds of times: You can't squeeze blood from a turnip.

If the vehicle is registered to another person, you might receive some money under the "permissive user" statute that makes a registered owner monetarily liable to a set amount for damages caused by someone driving her car with permission. If you can prove that the registered owner knew the driver had a history of drunk driving or was a reckless driver, the registered owner may be held financially liable for all of the damages under the doctrine of "negligent entrustment," that is, handing the keys over to a person she knows should not be driving. If the driver was employed and working at the time of the accident, such as transferring merchandise or parts between stores, you may have the right to sue his employer for your injuries and damage.

Depending on the situation, you may want to sue the uninsured or underinsured driver in court and get a judgment against him. Judgments are good in California for 10 years, and after that, they are renewable every 10 years until they are paid off ("satisfied"). That way, if the driver comes into any money—such as an inheritance—you will be able to collect from that.

Of course, finding a lawyer who will take a case in such a situation will be extremely hard, as the lawyer usually will not want to spend much time and energy chasing the wind and waiting for years for money that may never come. But before you decide against seeking compensation from the person who harmed you, regardless of how indigent he may appear to be, always consult an experienced personal injury lawyer, especially if your injuries are serious. The lawyer may know of various legal theories that can be used to get you a significant settlement or award from, say, the city for a negligently designed or maintained road, or the employer of the driver if the driver was running a business errand for his employer.

If you are injured by a driver who has no insurance, or has insurance but its limits are not enough to cover all of your expenses, you should be able to collect some or all of your damages and bills under the uninsured motorist coverage of your own automobile insurance policy, assuming you purchased such coverage. This coverage is highly recommended.

Uninsured motorist coverage is usually paired with underinsured motorist coverage, which kicks in after the other driver's insurance, if any, has paid its limits.

REPORTING THE ACCIDENT TO THE POLICE, THE DMV, OR YOUR INSURANCE COMPANY

Even if you were not at fault, you are generally required to promptly report the accident and your injuries, if any, to your own insurance company. One advantage to this is that, in an automobile case, they can arrange to have your vehicle repaired and provide you with a loaner car while your car is in the body shop. Of course, this applies only if you have collision insurance and you will be liable for the $250 or $500 deductible; however, you can recover that amount from the negligent driver that caused the accident.

If your accident is a slight "fender bender" and you have suffered no personal injuries and the property damage is minimal, the driver who caused the accident may beg you not to call the police or report the accident to the insurance companies for fear his insurance premiums will skyrocket. Even if you agree to this at the accident scene, ask to see the other driver's insurance information and write down the name of the insurance company, the policy number, and the name and phone number of the agent. Also ask to see the registration to verify that the person who hit you does indeed own the vehicle. If the person who hit you is not the registered owner, write down the information on the registration regarding the registered owner and her address. Also write down the year, make, model, and color of the vehicle, as well as the license plate number.

Frequently a driver doesn't want you to call the police and asks to work it out among yourselves because he doesn't have any insurance or is driving on a suspended license. However, if the other driver does in fact have insurance and you don't believe you were injured, a day or two later you may wake up with a stiff neck, back, and shoulders—typical soft tissue injuries that will require at least a doctor's evaluation and probably four to six weeks of physical therapy. What are the chances that the other driver will pay out of his own pocket not only the costs of fixing your car (which are probably considerably more expensive to repair than you thought they would be), but also the medical costs you incurred?

In such a case, you will need to report the accident to your own insurance company (if you haven't already) and to the other driver's insurance company, despite his earlier protestations that he would take care of the expenses out of his own pocket. Keep in mind that if there has been any personal injury or death arising from the accident, or property damage in excess of $750, the law requires that a form (SR-1) must be filed with the Department of Motor Vehicles within 10 days of the accident.

DO YOU REALLY NEED A LAWYER?

If your case is a typical fender bender that results only in damage to your car, you may be able to handle the claim on your own. However, if a day or two after the accident you feel some stiffness in your neck, back, and shoulders, you should make an appointment with your doctor or chiropractor for a checkup and see whether you suffered any soft-tissue injuries as a result of the accident. If you have such symptoms, the doctor may prescribe a course of physical therapy for you. At this point, the insurance adjuster, who was so friendly and nice to you, and so quick to get your car fixed, will now take a more adversarial attitude with you. The adjuster may claim that when you talked to her, you didn't have any problems in your neck, back, and shoulders and you're making it up to pad your claim.

If your injuries are relatively minor, you may still wish to pursue the case on your own and negotiate with the insurance adjuster. In the typical automobile accident involving moderate damage to the car and minor whiplash or other soft-tissue injuries to the victim, insurance companies generally use a formula to compute the amount of damages they will pay. Insurance companies will usually take the amount of medical expenses, multiply that by two or three times to determine "pain and suffering," add the amount of lost wages and property damage to that figure, and presto!—you have a settlement offer.

If you cannot come to a settlement agreement with the adjuster, you can sue in small claims court. If you suffer personal injury in addition to the damage to your car, you would be well served by making an appointment with an experienced personal injury lawyer to get a better idea of how much your case may be worth. Your damages may be more severe than you think and you may find yourself agreeing to let the lawyer handle the matter for you.

In the beginning, the insurance adjuster will be kind and nice to you, get your car fixed promptly and pay for a rental car, and may even pay for your doctor's initial visit. The adjuster will add up these bills, include a small amount for your pain and suffering, and make you an offer to settle the claim. Don't be fooled by the adjuster's kindness. She is trying to settle the claim as quickly as possible for as little as possible. If you mention the possibility of having a lawyer review the case to see if the settlement offer is fair, the insurance adjuster will tell you that you don't need to see a lawyer, that the adjuster is being fair with you, and the lawyer's fees will be coming out of your pocket so you will end up with less money in the long run. Don't fall for the insurance adjuster's line. Studies show that persons represented by a lawyer end up with more money in their pockets after the case is settled or a jury award is obtained than people who represent themselves, and this is after the lawyer's fee has been paid from the settlement or award.

SUING IN SMALL CLAIMS COURT

California small claims court lets you sue for up to $10,000.00. If your case is valued at $10,000 or below, there are a number of reasons not to hire a lawyer but to handle the matter yourself. First of all, it may be difficult to find a lawyer to take a case that is only worth $10,000. Second, a small claims court trial takes place only a month or two after filing the complaint with the court and serving the court documents on the defendant. Compare this with being represented by a lawyer, in which event the case may drag on for months, even a year or more, and you will not be significantly better than if you had sued the guilty party in small claims court.

11 MUNICIPAL TRANSPORTATION (MASS TRANSIT) ACCIDENTS

Each day, hundreds of thousands of people rely on public or municipal transportation to get to work, go shopping, visit friends, or to otherwise get from one place to another. Every year, thousands of riders are injured when the public transit car they are riding in gets into an accident with another vehicle, pulls away from the curb too quickly while a person is trying to get on or off the mode of transportation, or when a passenger loses their balance because of a violent stop or jerk.

Mass transit accidents happen for a variety of reasons. For instance, perhaps a bus is following another vehicle too closely and crashes into the other vehicle when it suddenly stops. Of course, as far as passengers are concerned, it is not necessary for the bus or other form of public transportation they are riding to actually crash into the other vehicle. If the operator of the public vehicle was able to avoid crashing into the vehicle ahead of it, the public entity may still be legally responsible ("liable") for injuries to its passenger who may fall or otherwise be injured due to the sudden stop.

Some other common causes of mass transit accidents are:

• Sudden acceleration

- Colliding with another vehicle when merging with traffic after making a stop
- Turning too suddenly or too quickly
- Improper maintenance of the vehicle (such as worn-out brakes that don't stop the vehicle in time to avoid an accident)
- Carelessness or recklessness of the driver or operator
- Inattention of the driver
- The driver being under the influence of alcohol or drugs (legal or illegal, prescription or over-the-counter)
- Wire derailment
- Equipment failure

The public entity has an obligation, both to its passengers and non-passengers alike, to hire only qualified drivers, operators, and other employees and to see to it that they are properly trained to do their job.

The liability of publicly owned or operated buses, the MUNI, light-rail systems, Metrolink, heavy-rail systems, subway cars, BART, electric trolleys, cable cars, trains, and other modes of mass transportation operated by a public entity (such as a city, county, the State of California, or the United States government) involves two "standards of care:" one to its passengers and another to non-passengers. In the relationship with its passengers, a government-operated transit system is considered a "common carrier," and so it owes those individuals a higher degree of care. Toward non-passengers, the transit system owes only the duty of ordinary care.

WHO IS A PASSENGER?

It is not necessary for the person to be completely inside the bus or other form of mass transit and to have paid the fare to be considered a "passenger." A person becomes a passenger when he demonstrates an intent to board the vehicle and the vehicle stops to let him on. A person who is in the process of getting off a public vehicle is still considered a passenger until he is safely off the vehicle. Thus, from the moment a person signals his intention to get on the vehicle and the vehicle stops to pick him up until he is safely discharged from the vehicle in a reasonably safe place, the public vehicle, as a common carrier, is required to use the utmost care and diligence for the passenger's safety.

Suppose a public bus pulls away from the curb while someone is trying to get on, resulting in the person's falling into the street and being run over by the back wheels of the bus. The public entity that owns or operates the bus can be held legally responsible ("liable") for the injuries to or death of that person (who is legally considered to be a passenger) for failing to use the highest duty of care for the safety of the passenger trying to board the bus, even though he was not completely inside the bus and had not paid the fare at the time of the injury or death.

A person is considered a passenger until he has safely gotten off the public vehicle in a relatively safe place. The public vehicle's operator's responsibility to the passenger continues until the passenger has had sufficient time to get away from the vehicle without injury. The public entity is legally responsible for any and all injuries a passenger suffers if, for instance, a public bus starts pulling away at a stop while the passenger is still in the process of getting off the bus, and he is injured when he falls when the bus starts moving again. The public bus is not necessarily required to let the passengers off at the curb; however, the bus driver must let the passengers off in a safe place where there is no danger of their being hit by passing vehicles or being injured by a dangerous condition of the street.

A special relationship exists between the means of public transit and its passengers that imposes a heightened duty on the public entity and its operators to safeguard its passengers. As the California Supreme Court has stated in relation to buses: "Bus passengers are sealed in a moving steel cocoon. Large numbers of strangers are forced into very close physical contact with one another under conditions that are crowded, noisy, and overheated. At the same time, the means of entering and exiting the bus are limited and under the exclusive control of the bus driver. Thus, passengers have no control over who is admitted on the bus and, if trouble arises, are wholly dependent upon the bus driver to summon help or provide a means of escape. These characteristics of buses are, at the very least, conducive to outbreaks of violence between passengers and at the same time significantly limit the means by which passengers can protect themselves from assaults by fellow passengers. We believe these characteristics of public transportation, along with the duty of utmost care and diligence imposed by California law, provide a more than ample basis for finding that a special relationship exists between buses and their passengers."

MASS TRANSIT AS COMMON CARRIER

A "common carrier" is a person, company, or public entity that basically agrees to transport anyone who can pay the fare (in legal terms, persons who "tender the price of carriage"). A publicly owned or operated mass transit system that transports passengers is a common carrier. As to its passengers, the public entity, as a common carrier, owes them the "highest degree of due care" and is liable for its passengers' injuries and deaths resulting from even the slightest carelessness ("negligence"). Common carriers are required to do all that human care, vigilance, and foresight can reasonably accomplish under the circumstances to protect its passengers from being hurt or killed.

As to non-passengers, such as people in other vehicles, motorcyclists, bicyclists, or pedestrians not intending to board the mass transit vehicle, the government entity owes them only the "ordinary standard of care." This is the duty to conduct its operations in such a manner so as not to put the people traveling via the other vehicles or pedestrians at an unreasonable risk of harm.

Being a common carrier, a public entity has a duty to use the utmost care and diligence to protect its passengers from assaults by other passengers. The public entity can be held legally responsible for injuries resulting from an assault by another passenger when the operator of the public vehicle knew or should have known that an assault on a passenger may be about to occur and had the ability to prevent the injury. This does not require that the public entity provide an armed security guard on every public mass transit vehicle. Rather, there are a number of precautionary measures the operator could take which would impose little, if any, burden on the operator. Some of the actions that could be taken include the operator: (1) warning unruly passengers to quiet down or get off the vehicle, (2) calling the police and asking for their assistance, or (3) ejecting the unruly passengers.

NECESSITY OF FILING A TIMELY CLAIM

One thing that is vitally important to know about injuries caused by a governmental agency or public employee is that, before you can sue, you must file a claim for damages with the appropriate governmental agency within a shortened period (usually six months). If you don't, you will forever lose your right to hold the public entity responsible for your injuries or your loved one's death. It is therefore extremely important that, if you want to pursue a case involving the fault of a government agency, you contact an experienced personal attorney as soon as possible.

12 LARGE TRUCK ACCIDENTS

A "large truck" is defined as one having a gross weight in excess of 10,000 pounds. According to the National Highway Traffic Safety Administration (NHTSA), in 2008, 380,000 large trucks were involved in traffic accidents in the United States. About 4,000 of the large trucks were involved in fatal crashes, resulting in approximately 4,250 fatalities. One of out every nine traffic fatalities in 2008 resulted from a collision involving a large truck. In addition to the people killed in a large truck accident, 90,000 people were injured in such crashes. In 2008, large trucks accounted for 8 percent of all vehicles involved in fatal collisions and 4 percent of all vehicles involved in injury and property-damage-only crashes.

Approximately nine million registered large trucks are on the road. There are two main categories of large trucks: (1) single-unit trucks, in which the engine, cab, drive train, and cargo area are all on one chassis, and (2) combination-unit trucks. A combination-unit truck is defined as a tractor pulling any number of trailers, or a straight truck pulling at least one trailer. In this configuration, a separate power unit is combined with a trailer. Conventional combination vehicles include a 5- or 6-axle tractor semi-trailer. The 5-axle tractor semi-trailer is the most popular configuration. It has a common maximum weight of 80,000 to 90,000 pounds when fully loaded and accounts for about 60 percent of all large trucks involved in a fatal collision.

When a large truck gets into an accident, it is rarely the typical fender bender. Because of the weight disparity between a large truck and the typical vehicle—be it a sedan or an SUV—or a motorcyclist, bicyclist, and pedestrian, the damage is usually severe and the injuries critical, even fatal. The average passenger vehicle weighing 2,500 to 3,500 pounds is no match for a fully loaded commercial truck weighing up to 80,000 pounds or more.

Of the deaths that resulted from crashes involving large trucks in

2008, 74 percent were occupants of another vehicle, 10 percent were non-occupants (e.g., pedestrians and bicyclists), and 16 percent were occupants of the large truck (that is, the truck driver himself or his passenger). Of the people injured in crashes involving large trucks, 71 percent were occupants of another vehicle, 3 percent were non-occupants, and 26 percent were occupants of the large truck.

Large trucks are more likely to be involved in fatal multiple-vehicle crashes (as opposed to fatal single-vehicle crashes) than are passenger vehicles. In 30 percent of the two-vehicle fatal crashes involving a large truck and another type of vehicle, both vehicles were hit in the front. In half of the two-vehicle crashes involving a large truck and another type of vehicle, both vehicles were proceeding straight at the time of the crash. About one-third of two-vehicle fatal crashes involving large trucks are head-on collisions. In 9 percent of the crashes, the other vehicle was making a turn. In 9 percent of large-truck accidents, either the truck or the other vehicle was negotiating a curve at the time of the collision. In 8 percent, either the truck or the other vehicles was stopped or parked in a traffic lane.

Fatal truck accidents involving large trucks are most likely to occur during the daytime (67 percent) on a weekday (80 percent) in a rural area (64 percent) on dry road conditions. On weekends, 63 percent of truck-related crashes occur at night (6:00 p.m. to 5:59 a.m.).

In addition to the injuries caused by the impact of the collision, there will be the possibility of serious secondary injuries in cases where the large truck is hauling hazardous or flammable materials. A victim may come into contact with or breathe in caustic hazardous materials. She may be severely burned or suffer smoke or heat inhalation injuries if the tanker trailer spills its load of gas or other flammable fuel and catches fire.

CAUSES OF LARGE TRUCK ACCIDENTS

There are four broad reasons large trucks get into accidents: (1) driver error, (2) something is mechanically wrong with the truck (usually a problem involving the brakes, tires, lights, or steering, often due to negligent maintenance of the truck or trailer), (3) there is a defect in the condition or design of the road or traffic signs or signals, or (4) there is a defect in the design or manufacture of the truck and/or trailer.

DRIVER ERROR

As for driver error, there are a number of reasons the driver may make a mistake. Common reasons are:

- Fatigue
- Speeding or driving too fast for the conditions
- Following too closely (tailgating)
- Unfamiliarity with the road
- Aggressive driving
- Changing lanes unsafely
- Being under the influence of alcohol or drugs (especially

stimulants), including drugs that are prescription or over-the-counter which affect the driver's concentration, reflexes, and judgment

- Lack of experience or training
- Misjudging the speed of other vehicles on the road
- Being distracted by something inside or outside of the cab
- Driving outside of designated truck lanes
- Making an illegal maneuver
- Not paying sufficient attention to the road ahead and traffic conditions
- Backing up without taking appropriate precautions
- Failing to signal a turn
- Poor performance during an accident, such as panicking, overcompensating, or exercising poor directional control
- The driver's working environment, including wages, pay basis (i.e., by the hour, mile, or trip), and company safety record

Driver fatigue may result in up to 30 percent of truck accidents. The driver may have compensation incentives that encourage faster truck speeds and more hours of consecutive driving than would be normally allowed or advisable. Unrealistic schedules and expectations of trucking companies often encourage drivers to hurry, despite the safety risks involved.

There are federal rules and regulations on the number of hours an interstate commercial truck driver may drive each week, as well as the number of hours of sleep the driver is expected to get each night. The driver is expected to keep a log of his activities, such as hours and miles on the road and hours and time of sleep. However, drivers frequently falsify their log entries or complete their log books days after the fact, ignoring the regulations while en route to their destination. Before President George W. Bush changed the rules, truck drivers could spend 10 consecutive hours behind the wheel, and could drive a maximum of only 60 hours each week. The driver could return to work only after 50 hours off-duty.

In the last months of his administration, however, President Bush signed a regulation increasing the number of hours a truck driver could drive each day from 10 to 11 and increasing the total number of hours the driver could drive from 60 to 77 hours a week. After the driver has driven the maximum amount of hours, the Bush regulation requires that the driver must not drive for at least 34 consecutive hours, 16 hours fewer than the previous 50 hours the driver was required to be off-duty. As a result of the Bush changes, drivers are driving longer hours on less rest, resulting in an increase in the number of big truck accidents. The percentage of fatal crashes resulting from driver fatigue rose 20 percent from 2004 to 2005, the first year in which the longer driving hours were allowed. In October 2009, the Federal Motor Carrier Safety Administration signed an agreement with consumer groups, the Teamsters Union, and others vowing to revise the 11-hour rule. With the increase in driving hours, many drivers resort to stimulant drugs to help to keep them awake and aware.

Nearly one-fourth (24 percent) of all large-truck drivers involved in fatal crashes in 2008 had at least one prior speeding conviction, compared to 18 percent of passenger car drivers involved in fatal crashes. However, drivers of large trucks were less likely to have a previous license suspension or revocation than were passenger car drivers (7 percent and 15 percent, respectively). Only 2 percent of large-truck drivers involved in fatal crashes had a blood alcohol content (BAC) of .08 (the limit for driving under the influence) or higher. For drivers of other types of vehicles involved in fatal crashes in 2008, the percentages of drivers with BAC levels of .08 or higher were 23 percent for passenger cars, 23 percent for light trucks, and 29 percent for motorcycles.

MECHANICAL PROBLEMS WITH THE TRUCK

Worn brakes and tires, faulty steering, and light problems are the major mechanical reasons for large trucks causing an accident. If the brakes are worn, the driver is not able to stop the truck in time to avoid colliding with the vehicle in front of it or stopping at the limit line of an intersection. Worn or bald tires also prevent the truck from stopping properly and reduce the truck's responsiveness in turns. Steering problems make it difficult, if not impossible, for the driver to control the truck, while burnt-out or otherwise inoperable lights fail to show other vehicles on the road that the truck is intending to turn, has applied the brakes, etc.

Other leading causes of large truck accidents due to problems with the truck or trailer include:

- The failure to inspect the truck each day before it is used
- The failure to perform regular maintenance on the truck
- The failure to install blind-spot mirrors
- Equipment failure
- Improperly loaded trailers
- Insufficiently secured cargo
- The failure to maintain current inspection stickers
- A tire blowout
- Driving empty trailers in windy conditions
- A defect in the design or manufacture of the truck or trailer

In one study, more than one-third of the large trucks inspected after a crash had maintenance defects that would have placed them out-of-service (OOS) if they had been inspected before the crash. Brake problems were found in 32 percent of the trucks, and violations of light/marker/signal regulations were present in 23 percent of the large trucks involved in accidents.

In July 2009, the National Highway Traffic Safety Administration (NHTSA) issued stringent new braking standards that will save lives by improving large truck stopping distance by 30 percent. The new standard requires that a tractor-trailer traveling at 60 miles per hour come to a complete stop in 250 feet, rather than the old standard, which required a complete stop within 355 feet. The NHTSA estimates that the new braking requirement will save hundreds of lives annually, and will also prevent many serious injuries each year. It is estimated to reduce property damage costs by over $169 million annually. The new regulation will be phased in over four years beginning with 2012 models. The new rule applies only to truck tractors and does not include single-unit trucks, trailers, and buses.

Large trucks such as eighteen-wheelers have the risk of jack-knifing if it is necessary for the driver to come to an abrupt stop to avoid a collision or make a sharp turn to avoid hitting another vehicle. Large trucks also pose a specific danger when they are making turns, as they must make a wider turn than the average motor vehicle and another car may not realize the danger and get involved in an accident.

Tragedy often strikes when the truck's brakes are worn and can't keep the large truck from running wild down a hill. The truck driver may be unable to stop at a stop sign or red light at the base of the hill, resulting in the runaway truck crashing into everything in its way, causing deaths, critical injuries, and tremendous property damage. Or the driver may not be able to negotiate a turn at the bottom of the hill, also resulting in personal injuries to those in its way, damage to property, and possible deaths.

DANGEROUS ROADS

Problems with the condition or design of the roadway or with traffic signs and signals are another cause of truck accidents. In those cases, the public entity that owns or controls the defectively designed or improperly maintained road may be found legally responsible for some or all of the damages. The roadway may be defective due to a lack of warning signs informing the truck driver of a sharp turn ahead (such as in the case of an off-ramp) or a downhill grade and the need to shift into a lower gear to prevent a runaway truck. If a governmental agency, such as a city, county, or state, is in charge of designing and maintaining the defective roadway, it is essential that you see a lawyer as soon as possible, as a claim for damages must be filed with the appropriate governmental agency within six months of the accident or your claim may be forever barred.

Roads may also be dangerous due to icy or wet surface conditions, the negligent design of off-ramps (such as being too sharp and not having any caution signs warning truckers to reduce their speed to a certain limit so they can navigate the turn safely without overturning), highway conditions and signals, lighting, and weather conditions. These factors can also be important in determining the parties liable for the collision.

DEFECTS IN THE DESIGN OR MANUFACTURE OF THE TRUCK OR TRAILER

Apart from mechanical problems that may arise with a truck or trailer through ordinary wear and tear, some accidents involving large trucks are the result of a defect in the design or manufacture of the truck. For instance, the truck's gas tanks may be placed in an unsafe location, increasing the danger to the driver and other motorists from a breach of the gas tanks, causing them to rupture and catch fire, inflicting serious injuries or even deaths.

A defect in the manufacture of the truck is usually due to the carelessness ("negligence") of a worker at the truck maker's plant or at a company that modifies the truck's chassis for a special use. For instance, a welder may not do a proper job of welding two metal plates together, causing the plates to separate while in use, resulting in injuries or deaths. Accident reconstruction experts are frequently able to pinpoint a defective weld or other problem with the truck. (See Chapter 21, "Defective Products," for a more detailed discussion of a defect in design or manufacture.)

INDEPENDENT TRUCK DRIVERS

One issue that often arises in large truck cases is whether the driver of the truck was an employee of the company whose load she is transporting, or whether the driver is an "independent contractor." If the driver is an employee of the company and causes an accident due to her carelessness ("negligence"), then the company she works for is on the hook for all damages caused thereby under the legal theories of "respondeat superior" and "vicarious liability." However, if the driver is an independent contractor, such as a driver who owns her own tractor and is free to carry anybody's goods, then ordinarily only the careless driver may be held legally responsible ("liable") for the injuries or deaths she causes due to her mistakes or her failure to keep the tractor in good working condition.

The company whose load was being carried is generally not liable for any injuries or deaths when the driver is an independent contractor. However, the company can be held liable if it was negligent in its choice of this particular independent contractor driver. For instance, if the driver has a history of accidents or traffic violations, the company may be held liable for the injuries and deaths caused by the negligence of the driver while carrying the company's product. Or if the driver had little or no experience in driving this type of truck configuration or the company's employees carelessly loaded the truck, such as in a manner resulting in it being top heavy, the company may be held legally responsible for injuries caused by the inexperienced driver or the truck's overturning because of the improper load. The company can also be liable for the carelessness of the independent contractor driver when it retains a certain degree of supervision or control over the driver. The company that owns the trailer can also be held liable if the trailer had worn or defective tires or other mechanical problems that contributed to the accident.

UNSAFE ACTIONS OF OTHER MOTORISTS

In many accidents involving large trucks and another vehicle, unsafe practices of the other driver are the cause of or a contributing factors to the accident. For instance, the driver of a car may try to pass a large truck on the right, not realizing that the truck has moved to the left in anticipation of making a wide right turn. Of course, if the truck driver does not properly signal his intention to make the turn, the conduct of the other driver may not be considered careless. Other examples of accidents that may not be due in part to anything the truck driver did or the condition of the truck include the other party: (1) driving alongside or behind a large truck in its blind spot so that the truck driver cannot see the vehicle, (2) changing lanes abruptly in front of a truck or merging improperly into traffic, which may cause the truck driver to maneuver or brake quickly, resulting in the truck's jackknifing, and (3) making an unsafe left turn by not yielding the right-of-way to an oncoming truck.

However, if both parties were at fault, then the legal doctrine of "comparative negligence" comes into play, which reduces, but does not extinguish, the injured party's right to recover monetary damages for his injuries and related expenses and losses. (See Chapter 2 for a complete discussion of your rights when both drivers are at fault for the accident.)

13 TRAIN ACCIDENTS AND RAILROAD CROSSING ACCIDENTS

PASSENGER TRAINS

Passenger trains such as Amtrak and Metrolink are "common carriers." As such, these train lines owe their passengers the highest degree of care and safety, and they can be held liable for injuries to and deaths of passengers resulting from even their slightest carelessness ("negligence"). The duty of passenger and commuter trains toward their occupants as common carriers is discussed in Chapter 11, "Municipal Transportation (Mass Transit) Accidents." Toward non-passengers, the train owes only the ordinary duty to act carefully and not subject those off the train to an unreasonable risk of harm or injury. Non-passenger-carrying freight trains owe persons that same standard of care, the ordinary duty to act carefully and not put others at an unreasonable risk of harm.

On a Friday afternoon, September 12, 2008, at approximately 4:30 p.m., a Metrolink commuter train traveling through the city of Chatsworth crashed head-on into a freight train, killing 25 people and injuring 135 more. Both trains were on the same section of a single track that runs from Chatsworth station—which is double tracked—through Santa Susana Pass. The line returns to double track again as it enters the Simi Valley. Three tunnels under Santa Susana Pass are wide enough only to support a single track; expanding the area to accommodate double tracks would be financially prohibitive. The line's railway signaling system is designed to ensure that trains wait on the double track section while a train is proceeding in the other direction on the single track. The Metrolink train would normally wait in the Chatsworth station for the daily Union Pacific freight train to pass before proceeding, unless the freight train was already waiting for it at Chatsworth.

This was Metrolink's deadliest accident ever, and the country's deadliest railroad accident since an Amtrak crash in Mobile, Alabama killed 47 people 15 years earlier in 1993. The investigation showed that, despite warning lights, the Metrolink train had failed to stop or move to an outer track before encountering the freight train. The preliminary investigation showed that an engineer aboard the Metrolink train was using his cellular phone to text message a teen-aged railroad enthusiast in the minutes immediately prior to the collision. The last message he sent was just 22 seconds before the two trains collided.

A complaint filed against Metrolink and its contractor who provided the engineers alleged that Metrolink knew locomotive engineers were using their cellular phones to make telephone calls and send text messages on the job, even though these actions violated railroad rules prohibiting the use of cell phones while on duty. Federal investigators said that the engineer, who was killed in the collision, was supposed to have stopped at a red signal just before a switching mechanism that would have guided the freight train to a side track. Instead, the engineer allowed the train to careen over the switch at over 40 mph, bending it badly, before colliding with the freight train on a sharp curve about a quarter of a mile past the warning light.

In addition to the engineer's alleged misconduct on the job

that led to the crash, investigators also studied the position of the warning lights, stating that the position of trackside warning lights could have increased distractions for the engineer. Several witnesses interviewed by a newspaper reporter stated that the signal was visible from the station, and the signal was green as the Metrolink train left the Chatsworth station just before the collision. The National Transportation Safety Board (NTSB) investigators tested the railway signal system after the accident and found it to be working properly. The signal system should have shown proper signal indications to the Metrolink train, with two yellow signals as the train approached the Chatsworth station, and a red signal at the switch north of the station.

The NTSB conducted a final sight distance test in which identical locomotives as those involved in the collision were brought together at the point of impact and slowly backed away from each other. They found that the trains' engineers could not see each other until less than five seconds before the collision.

Accidents such as the one in Chatsworth can often be avoided by the use of a system such as "positive train control" (PTC), a safety backup system that can automatically stop a train that runs a red warning light and thus frequently prevents collisions. The Federal Railroad Administrator told a reporter several days after the accident that PTC would have stopped the train before there was a collision. The NTSB member leading the investigation stated that she was convinced that such a system as PTC would have prevented the accident.

Note that the duty owed by a railroad to its passengers includes not only those who are actually onboard the train, but also to those getting on and off the train. Further, the heightened standard of care extends from the depot to the waiting platform.

In 1997, then President Bill Clinton signed into law The Amtrak Reform and Accountability Act (ARAA) which, among other things, limits the amount of money victims or their families can receive. Recovery is limited to $200 million per accident—for everyone involved. The $200 million limit is for "the aggregate allowable awards to all rail passengers" from any single passenger rail accident. That includes both economic damages (such as medical expenses and lost wages) and noneconomic damages (such as pain and suffering). It also includes any punitive damages that may be awarded by a jury for deliberate misconduct, although the ARAA makes it much tougher to win a claim for punitive damages. While the ARAA names Amtrak in particular, the $200 million limit is applicable to all passenger trains. Although $200 million may sound like a considerable amount of money, it really isn't, particularly in train accidents that have the capacity to injure and kill hundreds of people, as in the Chatsworth incident. The constitutionality of the $200 million aggregate limit has not yet been tested in court.

While in office, President George W. Bush signed legislation that would have prevented persons injured in railroad accidents from suing in state court, limiting them to federal courts. However, on his first day of office, President Barack Obama stayed that rule. The reason the railroads want the cases tried in federal court is because state court juries tend to be more generous with their awards when they find someone was at fault.

FREIGHT TRAINS

Freight trains can derail and overturn, rupturing hazardous material containers, causing a burst of toxic fumes to escape and form a cloud of substances dangerous to neighboring areas. People who are in the area of such an accident and suffer injuries or death as a result of breathing in the toxic substances can sue various defendants to recover adequate compensation for their medical expenses, lost wages, pain and suffering, and other injuries and damages.

For instance, in 2005, a Norfolk Southern Railroad derailment ruptured a tank car carrying chlorine, killing nine people. Derailments or other accidents that result in the emission of hazardous and toxic chemicals can affect thousands of people in the area. If a person dies from inhaling toxic substances, his survivors can bring a wrongful death action against anyone who was negligent in causing the accident. Persons and entities that might be liable in the case of a train derailment or collision include the locomotive engineers and conductors, the railroad company itself, any independent contractor that supplies workers to the train company, the company that maintains the rails, and the persons or entities that are in charge of managing the flow of trains along the tracks.

RAILROAD CROSSING ACCIDENTS

The United States has approximately 140,000 public railroad crossings (also called "level crossings" or "grade crossings"). Of these crossings, approximately 50,000 have gates, 23,250 have flashing lights, and some 1,250 have highway traffic signs, wigwag signals, and bells. In the early days, railroad crossings had a flagman in a booth who would wave a red flag or lantern to stop all traffic and clear the tracks when a train was approaching. According to the NTSB, more than 80 percent of public railroad crossings do not have lights and gates, and 60 percent of all railroad accidents occur at these unprotected crossings.

Preventing railroad crossing accidents has been a concern ever since the invention of the iron horse. A number of different techniques have been used. In the early days, when a farmer or shepherd was moving his animals across the tracks, the gate would swing open to allow the farmer and his animals to pass over, but the gates would form a protective barrier to prevent the livestock (and people) from roaming onto the railroad tracks.

All public rail crossings in the United States are required to be marked by at least a crossbuck, which is the sole warning device in many rural areas. A crossbuck is simply a wooden post with the words "Railroad" and "Crossing" attached to it at a 45 degree angle. More heavily traveled crossings are equipped with automatic warning devices (AWDs), with alternate flashing red lights to warn automobile drivers and a bell to warn pedestrians of an approaching train. Crossing gates block the approach of motor vehicles to the tracks when activated. Now many crossings are using four-quadrant gates to prevent drivers from going around the gate that only bars travel for the lanes they are driving in.

With the automatic warning devices (AWDs), about 30 seconds before the train gets to the crossing, the train trips a track circuit near the crossing, which triggers the crossing signals. The red lights begin to flash alternately and a bell mounted at the crossing starts ringing. After several seconds, the gates (if the crossing is so equipped) begin to lower, which takes five to ten seconds. Most bells continue ringing throughout the entire procedure—from the time the red lights start flashing signaling the approach of a train until the gates have returned to their full upright position. The bells on some AWDs stop ringing once the gates are lowered. Approximately 15 to 20 seconds before it reaches the crossing, the train begins ringing its bell and sounding its horn in accordance with federal rules. The horn sounds as follows: two longs, one short, and one long. The train continues to sound the horn until the engine occupies the crossing. If the automatic warning device is equipped with a horn, the AWD may provide the whistle signal instead of the train; however, the train must continue to ring its bell. Once the train has cleared the crossing, the gates (if present) begin to rise, and the bells (if silenced) may begin ringing again. Once the gates are back to their fully raised position, all warning signals, including the lights and bells, are deactivated.

Technology exists that could prevent many vehicles from trying to beat the train by ignoring a gate barrier and driving around it and onto the railroad tracks, where it could be hit by a train. For instance, a gate that is long enough to extend over both sides of traffic, or a gate that also covers both sides of the road would discourage many, if not most drivers, from trying to beat the train. A new device called a "StopGate" is made up of two extended length arms that block the entire width of the roadway and lock into a securing device on the other side of the road. The gate arms are reinforced with high-strength steel cable, which helps the gate absorb the impact of a vehicle trying to crash through it.

When a driver maneuvers around a lowered gate barrier and tries, unsuccessfully, to cross the track before the train reaches the crossing, it can be difficult to prove that the railroad was negligent in any way. However, passengers in the car who are hurt—or the surviving family members of a passenger who was killed in the accident—may have the right to sue the driver (or her estate in case of death) for negligence in not obeying the barrier.

Some railroad crossings become dangerous because of overgrown trees or vegetation or buildings that block the driver's view of the tracks and approaching trains until it is too late to avoid them. In other cases, warning devices such as gates, bells, and lights that are designed to alert drivers that a train is coming are either broken or not installed where they should be.

Carelessness ("negligence") of the railroad workers may also contribute to a railroad crossing accident. The train may be traveling too fast in a populated area, not giving drivers enough time to react and avoid a collision. This is particularly true when, in addition to speeding, the train fails to sound its whistle, leaving drivers unaware that a train is approaching until it is too late to take evasive measures. The train company may also be liable for failing to properly train its engineers, conductors, and other employees involved in the operation of the train, making their employees work long hours without sufficient rest, or failing to supervise and/or suspend employees who have a history of safety violations related to alcohol or drug abuse.

When the injured victim claims that the railroad crossing was dangerous because of its design, non-functioning or malfunctioning gates, signal lights, and/or bells, or other defect, be aware that if a governmental agency was in charge of designing, erecting, constructing, or maintaining the railroad crossing, you usually must file a claim with the appropriate governmental agency within six months or your claim may be lost forever. This is one of the main reasons you should contact an experienced personal injury lawyer as soon as possible after an accident involving an allegedly defective and dangerous railroad crossway.

RIGHTS OF RAILROAD WORKERS WHO ARE INJURED ON THE JOB

In most industries and professions, when an employee suffers a job-related injury, she is able to collect worker's compensation benefits, even if the employer was not at fault in any way. Indeed, the worker can collect worker's compensation benefits even if the injury was her own fault. However, the railroad industry is an exception to this. There is no worker's compensation scheme to protect railroad workers who suffer on-the-job injuries. This does not mean, however, that the injured railroad worker has no right to be compensated when he is injured.

In 1908, in response to the thousands of deaths and injuries of railroad workers in the late 1800s and early 1900s, Congress passed the Federal Employers Liability Act (FELA) for the purpose of providing compensation to railroad employees who are injured on the job. FELA allows injured employees to file claims directly against their employers where it can be shown that the railroad was negligent in some way and caused the employee's injuries. To recover under FELA, the injured employee must prove that his employer was careless ("negligent") in some way, and that negligence resulted in the worker's injuries. Negligence can be defined as the railroad's failure to exercise reasonable care toward its employee so as not to injure him. Examples of negligence include not providing a safe place to work, proper tools and equipment to do the job, or adequate training or assistance.

The doctrine of "comparative negligence" applies in FELA case. Under the rules of comparative negligence, if the worker was partly at fault for causing the accident, his recovery is reduced by the amount of his comparative negligence. Thus, if the railroad was found 75 percent responsible for the accident and the worker was determined to be 25 percent at fault, the worker's recovery would be reduced by 25 percent under the rules of comparative negligence.

FELA provides that the injured railroad employee may file a lawsuit in the state or federal courts and have a jury decide the damages to which he is entitled, if any. Generally, an injured railway employee has three years to sue his employer for damages. However, if the accident involved a train or track owned and operated by a governmental agency (such as the United States, a particular state, a county, or a city), a proper claim for damages must be filed with the proper governmental agency within six months of the accident or the right to sue the governmental agency is lost forever.

Unlike worker's compensation laws, under FELA there is no schedule of benefits that the injured worker is entitled to receive weekly or otherwise. Rather, there are elements of damages the injured worker can recover, such as past and future medical expenses, lost wages and loss of earning potential, permanency of the injury and effect on lifestyle, past and future pain and suffering, disfigurement, and emotional distress. A successful FELA personal injury or wrongful death case usually results in a significantly higher amount of recovery than if the victim or survivors had to pursue their claims under worker's compensation laws.

14 MOTORCYCLE ACCIDENTS

Motorcycles make up more than 3 percent—over 6.5 million—of all registered vehicles in the United States. There are almost twice as many motorcycles registered today as there were 10 years ago. Per vehicle mile traveled, motorcyclists are about 37 times more likely than passenger car occupants to die in a motor vehicle crash and eight times more likely to be injured.

CAUSES OF MOTORCYCLE ACCIDENTS

Approximately three-fourths of motorcycle accidents involve a collision with another vehicle, usually a passenger car. In two-thirds of such accidents, the passenger car driver violated the motorcyclist's right of way. The most frequent passenger car-motorcycle collisions involve the motorcycle proceeding straight through an intersection and the passenger car making a left turn in front of the oncoming motorcycle.

In motorcycle accidents involving another vehicle, 27 percent of all fatally injured motorcycle operators had blood alcohol contents (BAC) of .08 percent (the national and state standard for drunk driving). Forty-one percent of motorcycle drivers who died in single-vehicle crashes had BAC levels of .08 percent or higher. Motorcycle drivers killed in traffic collisions at night were more than three times more likely to have BAC levels of .08 percent or higher than those killed during the day. Seventy-two percent of the fatalities in the operator age group of 40-49 involved alcohol. Almost half of all fatal motorcycle-involved accidents have alcohol involvement.

The highest number of motorcycle fatalities involves people in the 20-29 age group, many of whom ride the "supersports" type of motorcycles: sleek and powerful machines that can reach speeds of 190 mph. Speeding is a main or contributing factor in many cases involving fatalities and injuries among this sector of the motorcycle riding population. The percentage of riders aged 40 and above who get injured or killed in a motorcycle accident has been increasing significantly in the last 10 years, and the number of deaths among this group is catching up to the 20-29 age group. Motorcycle accidents involving larger motorcycles with bigger engines have also been increasing significantly. One reason for this is the increase in over-40 men buying large cruisers—many of them Harley-Davidsons—for recreational riding on weekends and holidays.

Because of their vulnerability and the lack of safety features on motorcycles, motorcycle drivers and their passengers are at higher risk for more serious injuries than occupants of a passenger car. A motorcyclist is more likely to break bones, suffer head injuries, and sustain severe friction burn injuries in an accident, particularly if he was not wearing protective clothing. Fuel system leaks and spills are present in about 60 percent of motorcycle accidents, posing an undue hazard for fire and heat ("thermal") burns.

LANE SPLITTING

Suppose you are operating a motorcycle at rush hour, and traffic is "stop and go." You decide to ride in the space between cars. While you're doing so, a car makes an abrupt lane change, crashing into you or causing you to lose control and go down.

You suffer serious injuries. Can the driver of the car claim that you were at fault for "lane splitting" or "lane sharing?"

In California, a motorcyclist may drive between cars, whether the automobiles are stopped or moving, as long as it is safe to do so. Whether it was "safe" to drive between the cars is determined on a case-by-case basis. There are no hard and fast rules. However, the driver of the car may be negligent in failing to signal an upcoming lane change to warn lane-splitting motorcyclists of the impending danger. The car driver may also be negligent in failing to look in her rear-view and side mirrors to see whether any motorcycles were approaching from behind before changing lanes.

SINGLE MOTORCYCLE ACCIDENTS

A significant number of motorcycle accidents are single vehicle accidents in which the motorcyclist collides with the roadway or a fixed object. In accidents involving only the motorcycle, operator error is the main factor in approximately two-thirds of such accidents, the typical error being a slideout and fall resulting from over-braking or running wide on a curve due to excess speed or under-cornering. While such accidents are usually operator-caused, preventing the motorcycle operator from suing anyone for his injuries (unless there was a faulty design of the road or other condition of the road that caused or contributed to the accident), a passenger on the motorcycle generally may seek monetary damages for her injuries from the errant operator.

LICENSING, INSURANCE & HELMET LAWS

California law requires the operator/driver of a motorcycle on public streets to be properly licensed and insured. Statistics put out by the National Highway Traffic Safety Administration

(NHTSA) reveal that 26 percent of motorcyclists were riding without a valid motorcycle license in 2007. Without a valid motorcycle license, a person may not be able to obtain insurance for operating a motorcycle. Proof of insurance is required to be submitted to the Department of Motor Vehicles (DMV) when registering a motorcycle.

According to the NHTSA, wearing a helmet reduces the chance of being killed in a motorcycle accident by some 30 percent, and it reduces the risk of suffering a traumatic brain injury by approximately 65 percent. California law requires the motorcycle operator and his passenger, if any, to be wearing an approved helmet. In California, an approved helmet must carry the seal of the federal Department of Transportation (DOT).

If you were not wearing an approved helmet or not wearing any helmet at all when involved in a motorcycle accident, the person who was responsible for the accident can use this fact against you to reduce the amount of monetary damages for your injuries. For instance, if a helmet would have prevented 45 percent of your injuries, your failure to be helmeted at the time of the accident will reduce damages by that percent. This is known as the doctrine of "comparative negligence," discussed in Chapter 2. Similarly, if you were speeding at the time of the accident and the speeding contributed to the accident, your monetary award will be reduced by the percent that the speeding contributed to the accident. If your speeding was the sole cause of the accident, then you would not be entitled to any recover from the other party, and may indeed be held legally responsible ("liable") for the other party's injuries and damage to her vehicle.

NEGLIGENTLY DESIGNED OR MAINTAINED ROADS

Added to the inherent dangers of riding a motorcycle, the motorcycle operator must often deal with less than ideal road surfaces and various obstructions, such as uneven asphalt, potholes, poor surface conditions, bad road designs, and hazards such as blind corners, placement of light standards, speed bumps, low curbing, ruts, debris, uncovered drainage pits, and others. Where a defective design or condition of the roadway causes the motorcyclist to lose control of her bike and go down, suffering injuries, it may be possible to seek compensation from the city, county, or state that owns and/or maintains the road. You need to be aware, however, that if you wish to hold a state, county, or city liable for your injuries, a claim for damages must be made with the appropriate government agency within six months or less, or your right to sue the public entity may be forever lost.

15 BICYCLING ACCIDENTS

Millions of Americans ride billions of miles each year on bicycles of every type and description. Some commute to and from work on a bicycle; others ride street bikes for exercise or competitively; while still others love the thrill of off-road riding. Approximately 540,000 bicyclists make visits to the emergency room each year. About 67,000 of them have head injuries, even though they may have been wearing a helmet at the time of the accident, and 27,000 suffer from conditions that are serious enough to require hospitalization. 43,000 bicyclists are injured or killed each year in bicycle-motor vehicle collisions. Only 8 percent of bicyclists ride the wrong way on a road, but this accounts for 25 percent of motor vehicle-bicycle accidents. Seventeen percent of accidents involve bicyclists who have run stop signs or red lights.

Bicyclist fatalities occur more frequently: (1) in urban areas (66 percent), (2) at non-intersection locations (67 percent), (3) between the hours of 5:00 p.m. and 9:00 p.m. (30 percent), and (4) during the months of June, July, and August (36 percent). More than 90 percent of all bicycle-related fatalities involve a collision between the bike and a motor vehicle. In fact, the first documented car crash involved an automobile-bicycle collision in New York in 1896.

When a bicyclist gets into an accident with a motor vehicle, the bicyclist usually suffers severe injuries, if she is not killed. A 150-pound person is no match for a moving vehicle weighing several thousand pounds or more. If you survive such an accident, you may suffer broken bones, such as in your arms, legs, pelvis, or ribs, or severe internal injuries. You may even break your neck (quadriplegia) or your back (paraplegia). You may also suffer a traumatic brain injury (TBI) when your head hits the pavement or other surface, even if you were wearing a helmet at the time of the accident. In addition, you may receive severe friction burns to your body by being dragged by the car. You could suffer from significant scarring or disfigurement.

RULES OF THE ROAD

Bicyclists are generally bound to follow the rules of the road the same as motor vehicles. The California Vehicle Code requires that a person riding a bicycle at a speed less than the normal speed of traffic moving in the same direction must ride the bicycle as close as practicable to the right-hand curb or edge of the roadway, except: (1) when passing another bicyclist or vehicle, (2) when preparing to make a left turn at an intersection or into a private road or driveway, (3) when it is unsafe to do so, or (4) when approaching a place where a right turn is permitted. Likewise, when the road has a bike lane, the bicyclist must ride in that lane subject to the exceptions to riding at the right-hand side of the road.

A bicycle rider or passenger must sit on a permanent and regular seat attached to the bike. Riding on the handlebars, for example, is prohibited. If a passenger is four years old or younger, or weighs 40 pounds or less, the seat must have proper restraints to keep the youngster in place and to protect him from the moving parts of the bicycle. Minors—persons under the age of 18—may not ride a bicycle, non-motorized scooter, or a skateboard, nor may they wear in-line or roller skates, upon a street or roadway or any bike path or trail, unless the minor is wearing a properly fitted and fastened bicycle helmet that meets appropriate standards. This includes young children who ride on a bicycle in a restraining seat that is attached to the bicycle or in a trailer towed by the bicycle.

A person may not drive a motor vehicle in a bike lane except: (1) to park where parking is permitted, (2) to enter or leave the roadway, or (3) to prepare for a turn within 200 feet from the intersection. A person may not stop, stand, sit, or loiter upon a bike path or trail if such action impedes or blocks the normal and reasonable movement of bicyclists using the bike path or trail. When a bicyclist is traveling upon a one-way street with two or more marked traffic lanes, the bicyclist may ride as near the left-hand curb or roadway edge as is practicable. It is illegal to ride a bicycle upon a highway or sidewalk while the bicyclist is under the influence of alcohol or drugs.

CAUSES OF VEHICLE-BICYCLE ACCIDENTS

The leading causes of motor vehicle-bicycle accidents involve the motor vehicle driver's failure to use turn signals, see the bicyclist, or yield the right-of-way to the bicyclist when the motorist is making a turn at an intersection, onto a side street, or into a private driveway. Vehicle-bicycle accidents also commonly occur when the vehicle driver parallel parks on the side of the road and then swings the driver's door open without first looking to see whether any bicyclists are approaching. Likewise, pulling into traffic without checking for oncoming bicyclists is another major cause of vehicle-bicycle accidents. Other causes of bicycle accidents include: (1) hazardous road conditions, such as potholes, sand, and gravel; (2) road construction; (3) jaywalking pedestrians; (4) defects in the design or manufacture of the bike or equipment (such as in the bike's frame or helmet); or (5) faulty repairs by a repair shop.

If you or a loved one have been injured or a loved one was killed by a negligent driver or through other causes while riding a bicycle, it is critical that you don't throw away or otherwise dispose of the bike; it may be a crucial piece of evidence. It can show how the accident happened, and the bicycle would also be needed if it is claimed that the bike was defective.

ACCIDENTS AT NIGHT

Many bicycle accidents occur at night, when the bicycle rider is not readily visible to the driver of a motor vehicle. When a person is riding a bicycle at night, the bicycle must be equipped with appropriate front and rear lights and reflectors that can be seen by oncoming vehicles or vehicles approaching from the rear or side. The California Vehicle Code requires that, when operating a bicycle in the darkness, the bicycle must be equipped with all of the following:

- A front light that emits a white beam which, while the bicycle is in motion, illuminates the highway, sidewalk, or bikeway in front of the bicyclist and is visible from 300 feet in front and from the sides of the bicycle.

  Note: Instead of having a front light attached to the bicycle, the driver may wear a lamp or lamp combination that emits a white light that can be seen from a distance of 300 feet in front and to the side of the bicycle.

- A red reflector on the back that can be seen from 500 feet to the rear when the bike is directly in front of lawful high beams of a motor vehicle

- A white or yellow reflector on each pedal, shoe, or ankle visible from the front and rear of the bicycle from a distance of 200 feet

- A white or yellow reflector on each side forward of the bike's center, and a white or red reflector on each side of the rear of the center of the bicycle, unless the bike is equipped with reflectorized tires on the front and rear.

BICYCLE RACES AND EXPRESS RELEASES OF LIABILITY

Bicycle riders who participate in races are usually required to sign an express waiver of release of liability stating that they will not sue the owners, operators, sponsors, or promoters of the race if they are injured in the race. Will these types of releases hold up in court? If the release was valid and effective, you won't be able to sue the sponsors and others involved in putting on the race for your injuries. To be effective, a release must be a clear and unequivocal waiver of harm or death with specific reference to the defendant's negligence. A contract of release from negligence must be in clear, explicit, and comprehensible language, free of ambiguity or obscurity. It must clearly inform the releasor, as an ordinary person untrained in the law, that he is releasing the other party from liability for the releasor's personal injuries caused by the releasee's negligence.

The words releasing the defendant from liability must not be disguised in complicated legalese, but must be written in simple, clear, and unambiguous language understandable to the ordinary lay person. The release must be drafted so as to clearly notify the releasor of the effect of signing the agreement. The release must not be contrary to "public policy," which generally prohibits the defendant from releasing herself for conduct that constitutes aggravated or "gross" negligence, or intentional wrongful conduct.

Suppose that, instead of being injured, the person who signed the release is killed in the bike race. Does the release bar the rider's heirs from recovering for their damages? Probably. When a person signs a valid release that would have barred a lawsuit against the wrongdoer had that person lived, the person's survivors are similarly barred from bringing a wrongful death action if the risk that took the person's life was encompassed by a legally viable release.

16 PEDESTRIAN ACCIDENTS

According to the National Highway Transportation Safety Administration (NHTSA), a pedestrian is injured every eight minutes by a motor vehicle (approximately 64,000 people a year), and about 4,500 pedestrians are killed each year when hit by a moving vehicle. There are a number of reasons why pedestrians are struck by vehicles: speeding, driving under the influence of alcohol and/or drugs, improperly placed traffic signs, faulty traffic lights, and dangerous road conditions can all cause automobile-pedestrian encounters. But the number one cause of pedestrians being struck by a motor vehicle is driver inattentiveness. Other causes include disregarding a crosswalk, disregarding a traffic signal, disregarding a pedestrian already crossing the roadway, and failing to stop for a school bus that is flashing its red lights.

WHEN AND WHERE DO PEDESTRIAN ACCIDENTS OCCUR?

Crashes involving a motor vehicle and a pedestrian are highest among five-to nine-year-old boys, who tend to dart into the street. Accidents involving elder pedestrians (age 65 and up) are lower than most age groups, but older pedestrians are more likely to be severely injured or killed in a collision than younger victims. For instance, the percentage of pedestrian crashes resulting in death exceeds 20 percent for pedestrians over 75, compared to less than 8 percent for pedestrians under the age of 14. The vast majority of non-fatal crashes (86 percent) occur in urban areas, but the number of pedestrians killed on rural roads is double the rate of non-fatal rural crashes. The reason for this disparity is thought to be higher rural speed limits and a lack of sidewalks, paths, or shoulders to serve as separated pedestrian walkways.

Sixty-five percent of accidents involving pedestrians occur at non-intersections. This is especially true for pedestrians under age nine, primarily due to their darting out into the street. For ages 45 to 65, pedestrian accidents are approximately equal for intersections and non-intersections. Pedestrians 65 and over are more likely to be injured or killed while crossing the street in a crosswalk.

Pedestrian crashes are most frequent during morning and afternoon peak periods, when the volume of traffic is at its highest. Fatal pedestrian crashes often peak later in the day, between 5:00 and 11:00 p.m., when darkness and alcohol use are factors. Nearly one-half of all pedestrian fatalities take place on Friday, Saturday, and Sunday. Older persons are more likely to be involved in a crash during the daylight hours. The highest number of pedestrian fatalities occurs from September through January, when there are fewer daylight hours and more inclement weather. Child pedestrian fatalities are greatest in May, June, and July, thought to be due to the increase in the children's outdoor activities.

CROSSING THE STREET

Pedestrians have the right of way while crossing the street in a crosswalk. The crosswalk may be marked with paint, or it may be an unmarked crosswalk where two roads come together. However, when a pedestrian is crossing the street in the middle of the block and there is no crosswalk, this does not make the pedestrian open game to motor vehicles. The vehicle operator must still use "due care" to avoid hitting the pedestrian.

Of course, when a pedestrian attempts to cross the street outside of a crosswalk, she may bear some of the blame for the accident and the amount of her recovery will be diminished accordingly under the doctrine of "comparative negligence." In some cases, the pedestrian's failure to cross the street at a crosswalk is the sole cause of the accident, in which case the pedestrian would not be entitled to any compensation.

A pedestrian should always be alert to her surroundings and nearby traffic. If there is a sidewalk, the pedestrian should use it rather than walking in the road. If there is no sidewalk, then the pedestrian should walk on the side facing traffic. The pedestrian should also wear brightly colored clothes when walking on the edge of a road to make herself more visible to passing traffic.

INJURIES TO THE PEDESTRIAN

Because of the weight disparity between a human being weighing one to two hundred pounds and a motor vehicle weighing several tons, it is easy to see that, even in a slight accident, the pedestrian can be severely injured, even killed. The pedestrian may suffer broken legs or arms or serious internal injuries due to the impact. The pedestrian may suffer a spinal cord injury that leaves her a quadriplegic or paraplegic.

If the pedestrian is thrown to the ground, she may suffer serious traumatic brain injuries. If the pedestrian is dragged until the car comes to a stop, the pedestrian may suffer serious friction burns to her body. Of course, when a moving motor vehicle strikes a pedestrian, there is always the risk that the pedestrian will be killed due to the injuries suffered in the collision. The deceased victim's legal heirs have the right to sue the careless ("negligent") driver for the wrongful death of their loved one.

17 BOATING AND PERSONAL WATERCRAFT ACCIDENTS

Over 12.5 million boats of every size, description, and intended use are registered in the United States. They range from 8-foot handmade sailboats to 16-foot ski boats to 30-foot cabin cruisers to 36-foot sailboats to 100-foot and longer luxury yachts. A day of sun and fun through boating at the river, lake, bay, or ocean can quickly turn into disaster due to an accident that results in serious injury or even death to persons in or out of the boat.

Especially on warm summer days and long weekends, California's waterways become crowded with all types of watercraft ("vessels"), with operators having experience ranging from years of boating to first-timers who just bought a boat and paid scant attention to how to properly and safely operate the vessel. Statistically, your chances of being injured or killed in a boating accident are highest on a Saturday or Sunday in July, between the hours of 12:30 p.m. and 6:30 p.m.

Besides the various types of traditional boats, there are the personal watercraft (PWC), such as Jet Skis and the like, inflatable boats and rafts, pontoon boats, houseboats, speedboats, and airboats. The vessels are used for a variety of different pastimes, from fishing to skiing to pleasure cruising to around-the-world sailing to racing to white-water rafting and more.

Approximately 3,500 reported injuries and 700 reported deaths occur each year due to boating-related accidents. (The numbers of actual deaths and injuries related to boating accidents may be underreported because of the owner/operator's failure to know of reporting requirements, discussed below.) Injuries due to boat accidents can come from a variety of sources: (1) death by drowning, (2) brain damage caused by lack of oxygen due to submersion in the water, (3) severe traumatic bodily injuries inflicted by an unguarded propeller, (4) colliding with another vessel or fixed object, such as a bridge trestle, (5) being run over by a boat or struck by a PWC, or (6) the inhalation of a lethal level of carbon monoxide, to name a few. Alcohol use is the leading contributing factor in fatal boating accidents, accounting for nearly 20 percent of all reported fatalities.

Approximately two-thirds of boat-related fatalities are due to drowning. 80 percent of all drownings and other deaths in boat-related fatalities involved boats less than 26 feet long. 90 percent of the victims who have drowned in a boating accident were not wearing a lifejacket at the time of the incident. It is the boat owner/operator's duty to see to it that all passengers are correctly wearing proper-fitting lifejackets. The operator of the boat has a duty to see that there are a sufficient number of lifejackets for each and every passenger.

Most boating accidents are due to operator carelessness ("negligence"). Open boats without a cabin or skiffs are the most common type of boat to be involved in an accident. Personal watercraft (PWC) are the second most common type of water vehicle involved in accidents, followed by open boats with a cabin.

TYPES & CAUSES OF BOATING ACCIDENTS

The top five types of boating accidents are:

- Collision with another vessel
- Collision with a fixed object
- Skier mishap
- Falls overboard
- Capsizing

Many, if not most, boating accidents could be prevented by a skilled, attentive boat operator. In fact, most boating accidents are caused by the operator's negligence. Some of the most frequent operator-controllable causes of or contributors to boating-related accidents are: (1) operator inattention, (2) carelessness or recklessness of the operator, (3) operator inexperience, (4) excessive speed, (5) no proper outlook when towing a skier, (6) towing a person in an inner tube, (7) other person, (8) alcohol or drug use, (9) making a sharp turn; (10) overloading the vessel, and (11) violating the "rules of the road."

Other conditions may not be under the operator's control, but nonetheless may give rise to a lawsuit for negligence against the boat's owner/operator. For instance, the operator of the boat may have no control over angry seas, but taking the boat out in hazardous waters or during foul weather may constitute negligence and subject the owner/operator to a negligence lawsuit if the boat were to capsize and the passengers became injured or died.

The operator of a boat is legally required to know the "rules of the road" and how to operate the boat safely so as not to pose an unreasonable risk of danger both to persons in and out of the boat. The owner can be held legally responsible ("liable") for all injuries and deaths caused by another person the owner lets operate the boat without ensuring that the person has experience with and is reasonably skilled at operating the kind of vessel in question and is not impaired by alcohol or drugs. Seventy percent of reported boating-related fatalities occurred on boats where the operator had not received boating safety instruction. The lowest number of fatalities and injuries occurs among operators who have taken a course of instruction in boat safety by the United States Coast Guard Auxiliary.

DUTY TO INSPECT BOAT REGULARLY

In addition to knowing how to operate the vessel safely, the owner/operator must inspect the boat regularly to ensure that it is in good shape for the purpose for which it is going to be used, i.e., that the boat is seaworthy. For instance, for an 18-foot ski boat, the operator must inspect the hull, the steering mechanism, the throttle, and other parts of the boat to ensure they are in good working order.

In the case of a boat that will be towing skiers, inner tubes, other boats, and such, special attention should be given to the cleats to which the tow line is going to be attached. The boat operator will want to make sure that the cleats are securely anchored and do not pose a danger of coming loose and hitting someone in the boat or the skier or boat being towed. In motorboats, the operator must also check the fuel tank, engine, and other moving parts to ensure that they are in good working order and not likely to fail or cause a fire or other untoward event.

REPORTING BOAT INJURIES/DEATHS

Boat operators are required to report their accidents to authorities in the jurisdiction where the accident occurred. The report must be made within 48 hours of an occurrence if: (1) a person dies within 24 hours of the occurrence; (2) a person requires medical treatment beyond first aid; or (3) a person disappears from the vessel. If the only damage is to the vessels and/or property and it is $2,000 or more, or there is a complete loss of any vessel, the incident must be reported within 10 days of the occurrence. The owner is required to submit the report when the operator cannot. Note that the above minimum reporting requirements are set by federal regulations; individual states are free to impose stricter standards.

INSURANCE CONCERNS

If you own a boat, personal watercraft (PWC), or other vessel or watercraft, you should check with your insurance agent to make sure your vessel is adequately covered. See if the limits of your insurance are adequate to protect you in the event that injuries are catastrophic or the incident involves a death. If you don't have adequate insurance coverage on your watercraft, and if you or someone else operating your vessel cause injury or death to a third party, that person (or their heirs in the case of a deceased person) may be able to go after your personal assets, including your home and savings, to satisfy any monetary judgment a jury may have awarded. Even if the jury finds in your favor, without insurance it still will cost you thousands of dollars in lawyers' fees to defend the case.

18 "SLIP AND FALLS" AND "TRIP AND FALLS"

Tens of thousands of people are injured each year in "slip and fall" or "trip and fall" injuries. The injury may take place inside a grocery store, when a patron slips on a fruit or vegetable that has fallen out of its bin. Or the owner or manager of the store may have failed to put up a "Caution Wet Floor" sign where an employee has just cleaned the floor but it is still slippery and presents an unreasonable danger to customers, or employees failed to conduct and document regular "floor sweeps" to ensure that nothing is in the aisle that could pose a danger to customers.

"NOTICE" OF DANGEROUS CONDITION

A landowner or business operator must know or should have known of the dangerous condition on his land to be held liable. This is known in legalese as "notice." The notice may be either "actual"—the owner or an employee either created the dangerous condition or saw it or was informed of it by other people before the victim's fall—or it may be "constructive"—that is, that it existed long enough that the reasonably careful owner would have discovered it and taken steps to warn of or remove the danger. The victim has the burden of proving that the landowner had actual or constructive notice of the dangerous condition, and had sufficient time either to warn of its existence or eliminate the danger prior to the victim's slip or trip and fall.

The requirement of notice can be proved by direct evidence, such as the owner or an employee having created the danger or the testimony of other persons that they, too, had slipped or tripped, or, even though they did not slip or trip themselves, had notified the owner of the danger. Or the existence of the dangerous condition can be proved by circumstantial evidence, such as by a lack of the owner to have any sweep log or other evidence that the area was inspected for dangerous conditions in time for the owner to take remedial action to prevent injury to the victim.

Each case must be determined by its own unique circumstances; there is no hard and fast rule imposing exact time limitations. If the injured victim can show that the owner or an employee did not make an inspection of the area within a time period that was reasonable under the circumstances, an inference arises that the dangerous condition existed long enough that the failure to discover it was not reasonable. It is ordinarily a question of fact for the jury whether, under all the circumstances, the defective condition existed long enough that it would have been discovered by an owner or employee who exercised due care.

The exact length of time the dangerous condition must exist before it should, in the exercise of reasonable care, have been discovered and remedied, is not fixed and varies according to the circumstances. A person operating a grocery store, in the exercise of ordinary care, must use a more vigilant outlook than the operator of some other types of business where the danger of things falling to the floor is not so obvious.

The failure to inspect the premises within a reasonable amount of time before the accident gives rise to an inference that the defective condition lasted long enough to have been discovered and remedied. Allowing this inference does not change the rule that if a store owner has taken care in the discharge of his duty by inspecting its premises in a reasonable manner, then no breach will be found even if a person does suffer an injury. Many larger stores have a "sweep log" that requires an employee to inspect the aisles regularly for dangerous conditions and then sign the log stating the time the area was inspected and that no dangerous conditions were observed or, if there was a dangerous condition, that corrective measures were promptly taken.

TRIVIAL DEFECTS

When a person has been injured because she tripped and fell due to, say, a ridge created by uneven pavement or flooring, the landowner or business operator will frequently claim that the defect was trivial and he should not be held accountable for such a small hazard. The "trivial defect" defense is most frequently raised in trips and falls due to uneven surfaces in sidewalks and floors. The courts recognize that a landowner cannot be held legally responsible ("liable") for every minor imperfection on his property, even if the landowner knows of the defect. Accordingly, the courts apply the legal rule that it is impossible for a landowner to maintain heavily traveled surfaces in perfect condition and minor defects such as differences in elevation are bound to occur despite the use of due care by the landowner.

In determining whether a defect is trivial as a matter of law, the court must consider all of the circumstances. The mere size of the danger, ledge, or depression should not be considered in a vacuum. The court must determine whether there were any circumstances surrounding the accident that might have made the defect more dangerous than its mere depth. The court must look at the intrinsic nature and quality of the defect to see if, for instance, it consists of mere nonalignment of two horizontal slabs or whether it consists of a jagged and deep hole. Also, a defective condition that may be apparent during the day might be considered dangerous at night without proper lighting. Evidence that other people slipped or tripped on the same defect may be important to establish that the condition was in fact dangerous and that the landowner knew of the danger before the victim slipped or tripped and fell and was injured.

Defects that have been found to be trivial as a matter of law include: (1) a metal strip that protruded some one-eighth of an inch from a building's marble floor, (2) a quarter of an inch hole with a two-inch diameter in a chipped tile floor, and (3) ridges in a floor of one-half of an inch, three- fourths of an inch, seven-eighths of an inch, one inch, and one-and-a-half inches in height.

Defects that have been found to be a question for the jury to decide whether or not they were trivial include: (1) a quarter-of-an-inch piece of reinforcing steel (rebar) protruding from the top of a concrete tire stop, (2) a one-and-a-half inch depression in the sidewalk, (3) a five-inch pothole that extended to two feet when the victim fell, (4) a chuckhole two to six inches deep, (5) a hole two inches deep and ten inches square containing oil and grease, (6) a hole nine to eleven inches long, four to six inches wide, and two to three-and-a-half inches deep, (7) a six to eight inch puddle of syrup on a store floor, (8) a hole in a sidewalk five inches long, two inches wide, and up to three inches deep, (9) a ridge raised two inches above the sidewalk, and (10) a hole in a sidewalk twelve inches long, three inches wide, and two inches deep.

The seriousness of a defect is not determined by a tape measure alone. Any and all circumstances surrounding the accident which might have made the defect more dangerous than its mere size are taken into consideration. Among the factors taken into consideration include: (1) how long the defect has existed,

(2) whether the view of the defect was obstructed in any way, (3) whether the accident occurred at night in an unlighted area, (4) whether other persons were injured by the defect, and (5) whether someone else had notified the owner, manager, or an employee of the defect and a reasonable amount of time to fix or remove the defect had passed.

WHERE A DANGEROUS CONDITION IS OBVIOUS

There is a defense that is often raised in slip and fall cases. This argument is that the danger was obvious, and that the accident and injury were the victim's own fault because he wasn't watching out for his safety. The fact that a danger was obvious often is not, in and of itself, a sufficient basis for relieving the landowner or business owner of her duty to keep her premises in a reasonably safe condition. The dangerous condition must be considered in light of all of the circumstances.

For example, a store may place its displays and signs of sales at eye level or higher to capture the shoppers' attention. Such signs and displays are designed to catch the eye of the shopper and take her eyes off the floor in front of her while walking.

Even when the victim was partially at fault for failing to notice an obvious danger, this does not necessarily mean that he cannot hold the landowner legally responsible for some of his injuries. Applying the legal doctrine of "comparative negligence," the fault of the victim is weighed against (compared to) the fault of the landowner. For instance, if the landowner was 60 percent at fault for allowing the dangerous condition to exist on her property and the victim was 40 percent at fault for not noticing the obvious danger, then the amount of the victim's recovery is reduced by 40 percent. Hence, if a jury awarded the victim $100,000 but found he was

40 percent responsible for the accident for failing to see the obvious danger, then the victim's award would be reduced by

the percent of his fault (in this case, 40 percent); so, instead of receiving the full $100,000, the victim would receive only $60,000.

TYPES OF INJURIES/WORKING WITH AN ATTORNEY

If you have been injured in a slip and fall or a trip and fall incident, sometimes your injuries will be obvious, such as a broken arm or head injury. However, it is not at all unusual for injuries to take a few days to a few weeks to show up. You should contact an experienced personal injury law firm as soon as possible. The attorney often will want to send his investigator to the scene of the accident to inspect and take pictures of the dangerous condition, if it still exists.

The attorney or his investigator will also want to talk to any witnesses to the fall while the facts are still fresh in their minds. The attorney can also help with seeing to it that you receive a thorough physical and mental examination and treatment for any injuries resulting from the accident.

19 ELEVATOR AND ESCALATOR INJURIES

Every working day, millions of Americans who work in buildings that have multiple floors take elevators to get to and from their offices. Many apartment, condominium, and co-op residents use elevators to get to and from their units. And every day, countless Americans ride escalators to transport them from floor to floor inside retail department stores and malls.

There are approximately 600,000 elevators in the United States and 120 billion rides on elevators and escalators each year. There are 20 times more elevators than escalators in the United States, but the numbers of persons injured and killed by the two modes of transportation are about equal. This means that you are 20 times more likely to have an accident on an escalator as compared to an elevator.

ELEVATORS AND ESCALATORS AS "COMMON CARRIERS"

In California, it is well established that commercial operators of elevators and escalators are "carriers of persons for reward." This means that elevators and escalators are "common carriers." As a common carrier, the owner and/or operator of an elevator or escalator has a higher standard of safety and care, and can be held financially responsible ("liable") to passengers who have been injured by even the slightest amount of carelessness ("negligence"). The California Supreme Court stated that a higher standard applies to all persons who submit their bodies to another's control by which their lives or limbs are put at hazard.

California Civil Code section 2100 requires a carrier of persons for reward (a "common carrier," including commercial elevators and escalators) to use the utmost care and diligence for their safe carriage, must provide everything necessary for that purpose, and must exercise to that end a reasonable degree of skill. Civil Code section 2101 requires a common carrier of persons to provide vehicles safe and fit for the purpose to which they are put, and the common carrier is not excused for default in this respect by any degree of care. Accordingly, an elevator car or escalator must be in "safe and fit" order to safely transport its passengers.

California law requires a common carrier to use the "utmost care and diligence" for the safe carriage of its passengers. The owner/operator of an elevator or escalator is bound to use the utmost care and diligence that a very cautious person would, as far as human care and foresight can go, and they are responsible for injuries resulting from the slightest neglect against which human care and foresight might have guarded. Common carriers are not, however, insurers of their passengers' safety. An "insurer" of a person's safety is liable for all injuries and deaths arising from its acts or neglect, even if it was not negligent in any way; it guarantees that the person will not be hurt, regardless of the cause of those injuries. In cases involving common carriers such as elevators and escalators, it is necessary to prove that the owner/operator was negligent in some manner. This is true despite the fact that the owner/operator of the device is bound to the standard of the utmost care and diligence, and even the slightest carelessness would be enough to impose liability.

An elevator or escalator owner/operator is a common carrier only in regards to individuals who are using the elevator or escalator for the purpose of transportation at the time of the injury. For instance, children who are playing at the top or bottom of an escalator, and not intending to ride the escalator, do not get the benefit of the common carrier higher standard of care. This does not mean, however, that the owner/operator of the elevator or escalator does not owe any degree of due care toward the child. In such case, the owner/operator still owes the child the duty to exercise reasonable care, that is, the standard of care owed under general negligence principles, to keep the premises reasonably safe.

The owner/operator of the elevator or escalator may have a duty to protect children playing on the elevator or escalator, particularly when the owner/operator knows that other children have played on the elevator or escalator in much the same way while those who should have been watching them were busy shopping. Because the owner/operator knows or could anticipate that young children would play on or around the elevator or escalator, the owner/operator has a duty to take reasonable steps to prevent those children from being injured or killed by the elevator or escalator.

PASSENGER CONSIDERATIONS

If a person is in the process of getting on or off an elevator car or escalator, she is considered a passenger even though she may not be physically in the car or on the steps of the escalator. A person is considered a passenger until she has safely gotten off the elevator or escalator in a relatively safe place. The responsibility of the owner/operator of the elevator or escalator to its passengers continues until the passengers have had sufficient time to get away from the elevator or escalator without injury.

A passenger's motive for using the elevator or escalator is irrelevant in determining the common carrier's liability, and the common carrier owes the same high duty of care whether the passenger rode for pleasure or business. So if a passenger is injured by an elevator that she was taking for the sole purpose of getting to the top of a skyscraper to enjoy the view, and did not intend to transact any business in the building, she is no less entitled to a safe elevator than one who uses the elevator to get to an office to conduct business. Similarly, a department store visitor who is injured by a defective and dangerous escalator while "just looking" is owed the same high duty of care as a person who goes to the store with the intent of purchasing an item.

ELEVATOR INJURIES

Many elevator-related injuries occur when people are getting off the elevator and the bottom of the elevator is not flush with the outside floor. Sometimes the difference between the bottom of the elevator and the outside floor is a foot or more. More frequently, however, "trip and fall" injuries result when the floor of the elevator stops short of or overshoots the floor by as little as one or two inches. This can result in the person's foot being tripped by the uneven lip between the elevator floor and the outside surface, causing the person to fall and suffer serious injuries, such as a broken leg, arm, or hip, or hitting his face on the ground causing broken bones and disfiguring injuries, or striking his head on the ground, resulting in a traumatic brain injury (TBI).

Hand, forearm, foot, and lower limb injuries can occur when a person attempts to stop the elevator's doors from closing so he can board the elevator car. The doors may be closing too quickly or too forcefully, causing injury. Occasionally an elevator cable will break, causing the elevator to drop to ground level in a free-fall, seriously injuring or killing the passengers. Modern elevators are usually equipped with a safety brake system to prevent this from happening, but the safety brake system has been known to fail, resulting in catastrophic, even fatal, injuries.

Many elevator accidents occur on construction sites when workers are traveling from floor to floor. If the worker's employer installed the elevator and is the one in charge of servicing and maintaining it in a safe condition and the worker is injured in an elevator accident, the worker's sole remedy is usually worker's compensation benefits. But if another company (i.e., a subcontractor) installed the elevator and has the duty of maintaining it in a safe condition, the worker injured by a defective and dangerous elevator may be able to sue the elevator company.

ESCALATOR ACCIDENTS

It has been estimated that as few as 15 percent of escalator accidents are the result of "unsafe acts." The majority of accidents are caused by worn, damaged, or faulty equipment, many of which could be avoided with proper inspection, servicing, and maintenance. Unlike, say, a car, the mechanical workings of an elevator and escalator rolls are not easily accessible. This means that less effective techniques are often used instead of physical inspection. As a result, reliability is reduced and the potential for accidents is greatly increased.

Ordinarily, a passenger on an escalator stands and does not sit on the steps. When one considers, however, the enormous numbers of patrons of stores that use escalators as a means of transportation, one must conclude that occasionally someone will fall and her hand must rest upon the tread of the step either for a very brief time or for almost the whole descent, depending upon the force of the fall, the ability of the person to recover her balance, her ability in regaining her position, and similar factors. Children use escalators in great numbers, and their hands may be on the treads even though they have not fallen.

A department store, for example, invites not only people who are alert and nimble and adult to use its escalators, but all of its patrons, with the possible exception of those patrons whose age and infirmity would make any use or moving stairs hazardous. Under the duty to use utmost care required of a common carrier, the escalator must be constructed, maintained, and operated with the purpose and design to prevent injury to those whose hands do get into the treads.

Not surprisingly, a large number of the people who are injured while riding an escalator are young children. Young children do not have the same stability as adults and are especially vulnerable to falling and being injured at the slightest bump or shake of the escalator. Young children are frequently fascinated by the movement of the stairs and will attempt to put their fingers or hands between the moving stairs and the stationary rail. Young children also have a harder time getting on and off and escalator, often falling in the process and being injured.

Children under the age of five are exempt from the rule of "comparative negligence," as a child of such early years is legally incapable of realizing and understanding that his conduct may result in his being injured by the elevator or escalator on which he is riding or playing. In short, the young child does not appreciate the nature and extent of the danger and voluntarily encounters it without regard for his own safety.

Unlike an elevator, which has doors separating the moving car and its passengers from the stationary shaft, an escalator must move alongside a stationary balustrade. It is important that openings ("apertures") between treads and risers, and between steps and balustrades, be kept to a minimum in order to prevent a rider's hand from being caught between them.

LIABILITIES, MAINTENANCE AND INSPECTIONS

There are maintenance companies that service, maintain, and inspect elevators or escalators to ensure that they are operating properly and are free of conditions that might pose a hazard to persons using the elevators or escalators. Such a company can be held liable for injuries resulting from its negligence in inspecting, maintaining, and servicing an elevator or escalator. If the owner or operator fails to have the elevator or escalator regularly inspected for dangerous conditions, she can be held liable for injuries to or death of persons using the elevator or escalator that are caused by the unsafe condition of the elevator or escalator.

DUTY TO NON-PASSENGERS

As noted above, it is well settled in California law that commercial elevators and escalators are "common carriers" and owe a higher duty of care towards their passengers than is ordinarily required. However, as to persons not on an elevator or escalator, nor in the process of getting on or off, the owner and/or operator owes them only the ordinary standard of safety ("due care"). Thus, if a part of an escalator broke off and was thrown 20 feet, hitting a shopper, the legal and financial responsibility ("liability") to that person would be determined using ordinary rules of negligence law, and not the higher duty owed by common carriers, as the person was not a passenger on the escalator at the time of the incident.

SUING THE MANUFACTURER OF
THE ELEVATOR OR ESCALATOR

If the elevator or escalator was defective because it was not properly made or designed, and a person is injured or killed due to that defect, the injured person (or the next of kin, if the person was killed) has the right to bring a strict products liability lawsuit against the manufacturer, supplier, owner, and operator of the elevator or escalator. Strict products liability law does not require that the injured person prove that the manufacturer or other person had failed to use due care (was "negligent") in designing or making the elevator or escalator. All that needs to be proved is that the elevator or escalator was made or designed defectively and that defect was a cause of the person's injury. There is no requirement that a specific act of carelessness (negligence) be shown. For further information about suing an elevator or escalator manufacturer, distributor, or seller, see Chapter 21, "Defective Products."

20 DOG BITES AND ATTACKS

Over 4.7 million people are bitten or otherwise attacked by dogs annually, with 800,000 of them bitten seriously enough to require medical attention. Each year, roughly 370,000 victims go to the emergency room for treatment of injuries due to being bitten by a dog.

STRICT LIABILITY FOR DOG BITES

Section 3342 of the California Civil Code makes the owner of a dog legally responsible ("liable") for all damages suffered by any person who is bitten by the dog while in a public place or legally in a private place. The owner can be held liable for injuries from a dog bite even if they occur on the dog owner's own property, if the person who is bitten was on the property lawfully, such as in the performance of his lawful duty (e.g., a postal carrier or public utility meter reader). The dog's owner is also liable for any bites by the dog to persons on her property if the person was on the dog owner's private property with the express or implied invitation or consent of the owner.

Although California Civil Code section 3342 imposes liability against the dog's owner for its bites, this does not mean that the dog's owner cannot raise any defenses that may cut off or reduce her liability. For instance, if the person was pulling the dog's tail, kicking it, or otherwise annoying it, which led to the dog biting him, the person may be banned from recovery or the amount of his recovery may be reduced under the legal doctrine of "comparative negligence," discussed in Chapter 2.

YOUNG CHILDREN AND DOGS

Young children are the most common victims of a dog bite. Children are especially vulnerable to being bitten by dogs because they don't understand the danger involved when a person approaches a dog, even if they have petted or played with the dog before without incident. Almost 80 percent of injuries to children bitten by a dog are to their face, neck, and head. Even a small dog can inflict serious injuries on a defenseless child. Note that, generally speaking, a child under the age of five is considered by the law to be incapable of being comparatively negligent. So if a child under five years old is bitten or mauled by the dog, it is no defense that the child may have been teasing the dog, pulling its tail, or otherwise harassing the dog. Whether an older child is capable of understanding the risks involved in approaching a dog, petting it, pulling its tail, and so forth, is determined on a case-by-case basis.

INJURIES RESULTING FROM A DOG BITE

Dog bites can range from a superficial bite that does not break the skin to a fatal mauling by the dog. Frequently the dog attacks the victim's face, inflicting severe and disfiguring injuries. The dog may go after the arms and torso of a victim who is trying to protect himself. In many cases, it will be necessary to get a tetanus shot, and if the dog is not current with its rabies shots, the dog will have to be quarantined until it can be tested. If the dog is found to have rabies, the bite victim will have to undergo a series of painful anti-rabies injections to ward off the disease.

PIT BULLS AND OTHER DANGEROUS BREEDS

Certain breeds, such as pit bulls, have acquired a reputation as unusually aggressive and dangerous. In one study, the Centers for Disease Control (CDC) found that pit bulls and Rottweilers accounted for 67 percent of human dog-bite-related fatalities, with pit bulls being responsible for the greater share of fatalities. The term "pit bull" actually refers to several breeds of dog in the same family. Most laws specifically define the category of "pit bull" to include the American Pit Bull Terrier, the American Staffordshire Terrier, and the Staffordshire Bull Terrier, and dogs with significant mixes of these breeds. A few jurisdictions also include the American Bulldog and Bull Terrier as falling within the definition of a pit bull.

Pit bulls frequently attack without provocation or warning, and the victim may be a family member as easily as it may be a stranger. As a fighting breed, pit bull dogs were bred to conceal warning signs before an attack. For instance, they rarely growl, bare their teeth, or issue a stare before they strike. While some pit bull proponents contend that they are only dangerous to other animals, media reports show otherwise.

Some people take the view that the pit bull has a "locking mechanism" in its teeth or jaw so that once the jaw clamps shut, it is practically impossible to get the dog to release its prey. Pit bulls often show "bite, hold, and shake" behavior when biting a person or other animal. Accordingly, some pit bull rescue organizations and advocacy groups recommend that owners of pit bulls carry a "break stick" with them to lever the dog's jaws open if the dog does bite and clamp down on a person or another animal.

Some cities have passed laws prohibiting the ownership of pit bulls and certain other dangerous breeds, such as Rottweilers and Doberman Pinschers. Some laws prohibit these breeds of dogs from going into certain public areas, and other laws require that the dog be muzzled when out in public.

Accordingly, if you have been seriously injured or a loved one killed by a dog belonging to one of these dangerous breeds, the insurance company is more likely to settle the case and to settle for a higher amount than if, say, a Collie or Springer Spaniel inflicted the damage. (Generally speaking, the amount of damage a Collie or Springer Spaniel can inflict pales in comparison to what pit bulls, Rottweilers, hybrid wolves, and Doberman Pinschers can do.) Also, because of the severe injuries they can cause—such as serious damage to the face requiring extensive reconstructive surgery—it is important that you obtain a law firm with experience in dog bite cases to help arrange that you get the best medical care possible for your often disfiguring injuries. In severe maulings, plastic surgeon and other medical expenses can run into tens, even hundreds of thousands of dollars in reconstructive surgery, such as skin grafting, tissue expansion, and scar diminishment.

LEASH LAWS

Let's say that you are walking down the street and a playful dog comes bounding toward you and jumps on you, knocking you to the ground, causing a broken limb, or hip or head injuries. Most cities and counties have laws requiring dogs to be on leashes and under the control of their owner or walker when off the owner's or caretaker's private property. The fact that this is the first time the dog has ever done something like this is no defense. The failure to have the dog on a leash, resulting in the dog causing injury, is called in legal terms "negligence per se." It is not a defense to a violation of the leash law that the dog is trained to obey verbal commands or hand signals. Nor is it necessary for the victim to prove that the owner knew that her dog had a propensity to run at large, chase bicycles, or jump on strangers to hold her liable for injuries caused by her dog while it was running loose throughout the neighborhood.

LIABILITY OF A LANDLORD FOR INJURIES FROM A TENANT'S DOG

A landlord generally is not liable for the injuries inflicted by his tenants' dogs (or other animals), unless the landlord has actual knowledge of the presence of the tenant's dog and its vicious nature. If the landlord knows of the vicious propensities of the dog and has the ability under the lease to order it removed or to terminate the lease altogether, the landlord may be held liable for allowing the dangerous dog to remain on the property without doing anything about it. For instance, if the landlord knows that a tenant on a month-to-month lease has a dangerous dog, the landlord may be required to give the tenant notice either to get rid of the dog or, if that fails, give the tenant notice of termination of the lease.

THE "VETERINARIAN'S RULE"

A veterinarian, kennel operator, or her employees generally are barred by the "veterinarian's rule" from suing the owner of a dog for bites or other injuries inflicted by a dog while under their care. According to the veterinarian's rule, a veterinarian or other person who by his profession works with dogs and other animals is held to have assumed the risk that he may be bitten or otherwise harmed by the animal.

21 DEFECTIVE PRODUCTS

Millions of Americans are injured or killed each year due to defective, faulty products that are dangerous even when being used for their intended purposes. Unlike other types of cases, such as automobile accidents or "slip and fall" cases, it is not necessary to prove that the manufacturer, distributor, or retailer of the product—or anyone else involved in the "stream of commerce"—was careless ("negligent") in designing or making the product. Rather, the manufacturer, distributor, or retailer is "strictly liable" for injuries, deaths, and damage to other property caused by a product that is dangerous because of a defect in its design or manufacture when it is being used for an intended or "foreseeable" use.

The rationale behind holding a manufacturer, distributor, or retailer strictly liable for a defective product without regard to whether it was negligent or not is that the manufacturer and others in the stream of commerce are in a better position to protect themselves from the costs associated with a defective product than are the users of the product. For instance, the manufacturer, distributor, or retailer can obtain insurance to protect themselves and spread the cost of the insurance premiums across the board by raising the price of its product a few cents or dollars. Putting the brunt of liability for defective products on the manufacturer, wholesaler, or retailer simply makes this part of its cost of doing business that it can pass along to the purchasers of its product.

WHAT IS A PRODUCT?

The definition of "product" is expansive. Products include everything from automobiles to bottles to elevators to mass-produced residential homes and apartment buildings. But it is not necessary that the product be mass-produced. The fact that a product is unique does not render its maker, distributor, or seller any less liable for any injuries or damage caused by it if the product is defective, if the company is otherwise in the business of manufacturing and selling products as part of its full-time commercial activity. Thus, a company that makes a one-of-a-kind device for a customer is bound by the laws of strict liability. Indeed, some companies are in the business of making specialized products for each job. This does not make them any less subject to the laws of strict product liability.

Strict product liability, however, does not apply to the one-time or occasional seller. For instance, if you hold a yard sale and sell an item that turns out to be defective and causes injury, you are not held strictly liable for the victim's injuries. The victim will have to prove that you were somehow negligent in causing the defect that injured her. Proving negligence requires a much higher standard of proof than strict liability. (Used goods sold by non-dealers are usually "as is" sales, and come with no warranties or guarantees.) Similarly, if a neighbor sells you a one-time batch of tomato sauce, he would not be considered a "seller" under products liability law. If you became sick after eating the sauce, you would have to prove that your neighbor was careless ("negligent") in making the sauce, and such negligence was the cause of your injuries.

WHO IS LIABLE?

A person or entity involved in the manufacturing, distributing, or retailing of a product is strictly liable if: (1) the person or company places the product on the market, (2) the person or company knows that it is to be used without inspection for defects, (3) the product proves to have a defect, and (4) the defect causes injury to a person or damage to property. The defective product must be dangerous and unsafe when used not only for its intended purpose, but also for uses that can be reasonably anticipated by the manufacturer, distributor, or retailer of the product ("foreseeable" uses).

A product may be defective because of a flaw in its design or a defect in its manufacture. The difference between a product that is defectively designed and one that is defectively manufactured is that, in the first case (i.e., design defects), all of the products—even if made to the manufacturer's exact specifications—are defective and dangerous. When a product is dangerous because of its design, then all products of that type are dangerous and the product is subject to recall, and a warning is given not to use the product and to take it back to the place where you bought it for a full refund.

On the other hand, when there is a defect in manufacture, that means that the product, when properly made, is safe for its intended use, but due to a mistake in its fabrication or assembly, the specific individual product is defective and dangerous. A common type of error that makes an individual product unsafe is a faulty weld. If welded properly, the product is safe for use, but if welded improperly, the product poses an unreasonable risk of harm to users of the product and persons nearby.

DEFECTS IN DESIGN

Mass injuries can result when products are mass produced but defectively designed in a manner that makes them dangerous when used in their proper way. A product is defective in design if either: (1) the product fails to perform safely as an ordinary consumer would expect when the product is used in an intended or reasonably foreseeable manner or (2) the risks inherent in the dangerous design outweigh the product's benefits. The first test is known as the "consumer expectation" test, while the second test is known as the "risk-benefit" test.

Under the consumer expectation test, when a product fails to meet an ordinary consumer's expectations as to the safety of the product in its intended or reasonably foreseeable use, a manufacturer is strictly liable for the resulting injuries or property damage. The consumer expectation test is based on the theory that when a manufacturer places a product on the market, it makes an implied representation that the product is safe for the tasks it was designed to accomplish.

The risk-benefit test of a defective design involves a balancing of the danger posed by the product's design against the product's usefulness ("utility"). This doesn't necessarily require that the product's risk of harm outweigh the product's benefits. Liability may be imposed where the product's design has an "excessive preventable danger," and it would have been feasible for the manufacturer to reduce the risk of harm by using an alternate, safer design. For example, a glass bottle of apple juice marketed for infant use could be made safer by an alternative design, such as the use of plastic instead of glass, thereby preventing injuries to infants who might be injured by broken glass if the bottle was accidentally dropped.

DEFECTS IN MANUFACTURE

A product is defective in its making when something happens during the manufacturing process that makes the particular item unsafe and dangerous, even though it has been designed safely. Some of the problems could be a faulty weld, lose or missing screws or bolts, or the use of materials that are inferior in quality to those called for by the specifications. The manufacturer or supplier of a defective part that is used in the product (a "component product") is strictly liable for any and all injuries and damages caused by its defective part, even though it is incorporated into a larger product.

CHANGES TO THE PRODUCT AND LIABILITY OF RAW MATERIAL SUPPLIERS

One major criteria of strict product liability law is that, at the time of the injury, the product was in substantially the same condition as it was when it left the manufacturer. If the company was in the business of supplying raw materials that would be incorporated into the final product, the questions then are whether the raw material met the specifications the manufacturer set and whether the product was materially changed. If the manufacturer ordered raw material of quality "A" but the supplier sent an inferior quality of product, the supplier can be held liable for strict product liability. If the supplier sends product meeting the standard requested by the manufacturer, but the design is faulty in not requiring a higher standard of raw material, the supplier is not strictly liable.

If what was sent by the supplier is a dangerous material in and of itself, the supplier can be held liable under the laws of strict product liability if the material retains its inherent quality. The most common example of this is asbestos. For years, asbestos was used by many manufacturers in a number of products and in many of them the raw asbestos was processed, yet the asbestos (particularly its dust) retained its toxic qualities. In such a case, the supplier of the raw asbestos is held strictly liable for injuries resulting from the inhalation of asbestos dust.

A product may also be defective when, although the product was properly designed and manufactured, it fails to include adequate instructions for its use or sufficient warnings regarding its dangers when used in a proper or foreseeable way.

IMPROPER USE OF PRODUCTS BY CONSUMERS

Note that the law does not impose absolute liability. If the consumer were using a product in a way the manufacturer, distributor, or retailer could not have foreseen, strict products liability does not apply. Also, where the victim was partially at fault for his injuries or death, the legal doctrine of "comparative fault" applies to reduce the amount of monetary damages the manufacturer, distributor, or retailer must pay. The fault of the victim is weighed against (compared to) the fault of the manufacturer, distributor, or retailer.

For instance, if the victim was 25 percent at fault for causing his injuries, then the amount of his financial recovery is reduced by that amount. Hence, if a jury concluded that the total damages amounted to $100,000 but found that the victim was 25 percent responsible for the accident, then the victim's award would be reduced by the percent of his fault (in this case, 25 percent), so that instead of receiving the full $100,000, the victim would receive only $75,000.

INJURIES CAUSED BY A DEFECTIVE PRODUCT

Sometimes when a person is injured by a defective and dangerous product, her injuries will be obvious, such as a broken arm, burns, or head injuries. However, in some cases, it is not at all unusual for injuries to take a few days to a few weeks—even years in the case of asbestosis—to show up. Therefore you should contact an experienced personal injury law firm as soon as possible after the accident. The attorney is familiar with the types of injuries that may arise as a result of being injured by a defective product, and oftentimes can help find a skilled doctor to treat you.

RETAIN THE PRODUCT AND ALL DOCUMENTATION

If you have been injured or a loved one killed by a defective product, you should promptly consult an experienced personal injury law firm. The defective property should not be reused, repaired, destroyed, or otherwise changed or disposed of without first giving the attorney and her investigator the opportunity to inspect and evaluate it. All instructions, warnings, other packaging materials (such as the box the product came in, if any), and receipts and warranties should not be thrown out, but rather given to the attorney so she can evaluate the sufficiency of assembly instructions, danger warnings, and other important information. The attorney or her investigator will want to talk to any witnesses of the incident while the facts are still fresh in their minds.

In most products liability cases, the attorney will want to keep the product in the same condition it was in when it caused the injuries until the case is completely over. In many cases, the attorney will want to hire an expert the appropriate certain field to evaluate the defective product and testify at trial. The attorney will often need to have the product and/or assembly instructions or warnings evaluated by a professional such as an engineer or human factors expert to see whether the product posed an unreasonable risk of harm. For instance, if a product failed because of metal fatigue and caused serious injuries, the attorney will likely want to have the product tested and evaluated by a metallurgist.

22   MEDICAL MALPRACTICE

Medical malpractice involves the negligence of a physician or surgeon, or anyone else in the business of providing physical and mental health care services. The error may be one in diagnosis, such as where the doctor misses or misinterprets ("misdiagnoses") a condition as benign rather than the beginnings of a serious problem. Sometimes the error is obvious, such as when the surgeon mistakenly removes a healthy kidney rather than the diseased one. Sometimes the malpractice is more subtle, such as where the doctor fails to heed the warning signs of diabetes and treat the patient with medication and exhort her to check her blood sugar frequently, watch her diet, lose weight, and/or exercise more. Expert testimony of physicians or surgeons in the same field of medicine as the doctor you are suing are usually necessary to prove the degree ("standard") of care and how the physician deviated from it.

ELEMENTS OF A SUCCESSFUL MEDICAL MALPRACTICE CASE

Three elements need to be proved to be successful in a medical malpractice case:

1. The victim must prove what the "standard of care" was; that is, what would a reasonable doctor acting under the same or similar circumstances in the same or similar locality have done?

2. The victim must prove that the doctor failed to meet the standard of care, in that his conduct was below the acceptable standard of care of other doctors acting under the same or similar circumstances.

3. The victim (or her heirs) must prove that she was injured or killed due to the health care provider's negligence.

LIMITATION ON DAMAGES

Most good medical malpractice lawyers will not take a medical malpractice case unless he believes it is a meritorious case and is worth at least $500,000 or more. The reason for this limitation is a law that was passed back in 1975, known as the Medical Injury Compensation Reform Act of 1975 (usually referred to by its acronym, MICRA). MICRA has several provisions that make it harder to sue negligent physicians, surgeons, hospitals, and other health care providers. For instance, although you can collect in full for all of your medical expenses, past and future, and all of your lost wages and loss of earning power (so-called "economic damages"), the most you can recover for so-called "non-economic damages" such as pain and suffering and loss of enjoyment of life is only $250,000. The statute also limits the amount of fees the lawyer may charge for representing you, which is less than what he could charge in other types of personal injury and wrongful death cases.

MICRA was passed during a time when doctors were complaining about the sudden and steep increases to their malpractice insurance premiums. Insurance companies said the rise was justified due to the number of frivolous cases brought by unscrupulous, smooth talking attorneys who could sway and convince a jury that the doctor made a mistake and that the client had suffered an astronomical amount of financial and medical expenses and had undergone severe and prolonged pain and suffering. The insurance companies conveniently avoided bringing up the facts that they were suffering because of some bad investment and underwriting practices they had made, and the cyclical nature of personal injury payouts.

Another reason medical malpractice lawyers are hesitant to take cases worth less than $500,000 is that it takes a lot of time and money to prosecute a medical malpractice case through trial. Medical malpractice cases often turn into an expensive "battle of the experts." The injured victim's expert doctor will say it was malpractice, while the defendant doctor's expert witnesses will testify that the care was proper and appropriate. The lay jury—most of them unschooled in medical matters—are left to make heads or tails out of the experts' testimony. In most cases, especially those dealing with complex medical or surgical issues, the jury will believe the doctor who comes across as the most knowledgeable and confident of all the expert witnesses, rather than trying to sort out and deal with the technical medical testimony itself.

Doctors have long looked out for each other, one major reason being that if they were ever accused of malpractice themselves, they would not want any of their fellow colleagues to testify against them. Accordingly, a code or "conspiracy of silence" among the medical profession arose and existed as early as the start of the 20th century. Thus, in medical malpractice cases, it is often necessary to bring in an out-of-town doctor who is familiar with the medical standards of the area in which the defendant doctor was practicing.

Doctors charge high fees to review medical records to determine whether or not there was malpractice, and their fees for testimony at a deposition or trial is exorbitant. Indeed, some doctors make a very lucrative living just acting as experts in medical malpractice cases. It is much easier for the defendant doctor—whose malpractice insurance carrier is paying the bills—to get doctors to testify on his behalf.

23 AMUSEMENT PARKS AND TRAVELING CARNIVAL RIDES

Millions of Californians and out-of-state visitors annually visit the Golden State's permanent amusement parks, such as Disneyland, Magic Mountain, Universal Studios, and Knott's Berry Farm, and go on amusement rides. In addition to visiting permanent amusement parks, millions of people visit annual county fairs or other traveling carnivals that bring with them a mobile midway equipped with dozens of amusement rides for young and old. Then there are church fairs and private birthday parties where people rent inflatable slides and "moon bounce" castles for youngsters to frolic on.

Unfortunately, a significant number of people are seriously injured or killed by amusement park or carnival rides that malfunction because of faulty operation; operator inattentiveness or carelessness; faulty design, construction, or maintenance; or lack of warnings regarding the required age, height, weight, and medical condition of a prospective rider.

Some amusement ride users are injured when they are thrown from their car because of the lack of a safety bar or a defective seat belt, or the car itself may detach from the ride causing serious injury to or even death of the riders or other fairgoers who are walking or standing in the area. In some cases, the rider is killed because of a defective ride or the negligence of the owner or operator in inspecting and maintaining the ride every day to ensure its safety.

Sometimes a rider who is injured because the ride isn't in safe working condition will escape with only a few bumps and bruises. A number of others, however, will lose fingers or toes, a hand or foot, or even an arm or leg if the limb gets trapped in a tight space while the ride is moving. Or they may suffer broken bones, such as in an arm or leg. Some riders who get into an accident with a faulty amusement or recreational ride may sustain an injury to their spinal cord that leaves them paralyzed from the neck down ("quadriplegic") or paralyzed from the waist down ("paraplegic"). Some riders will be killed due to a defective amusement ride.

At times, riders—especially those who ride the high-speed roller coasters and similar "thrill" rides—suffer traumatic brain injury (TBI, discussed in depth in Chapter 30) as a result of the ride. Severe TBI can result even if the rider didn't strike his head on anything during the course of the ride. Rather, the force of the violent shaking of some rides is enough to result in severe TBI by causing the rider's brain to move around and hit the inside of the skull. Often, a person who has ridden on a thrill ride will get off the ride feeling dizzy or nauseous. These are symptoms of possible serious brain injury and the person should be checked out by a physician (not just the park's nurse) as soon as possible to prevent serious brain injury. (This method of brain injury is the same mechanism that works to cause brain damage in "shaken baby syndrome," when the child isn't struck but is violently shaken back-and-forth and from side-to-side.)

LAWS PERTAINING TO AMUSEMENT RIDES

There is no single government body that oversees all types of amusement rides throughout the United States. The U.S.

Consumer Products Safety Commission (CPSC) has jurisdiction over traveling carnival rides, like the kind that follow county fairs throughout the state. The CPSC does not have jurisdiction over permanent amusement parks or water parks. The CPSC does, however, have jurisdiction over inflatable rides, such as inflatable slides and bounces.

Unlike the federal government, California has many rules and regulations regarding most permanent amusement parks and rides therein to ensure that they are safe and will not subject the riders to an undue risk of harm. The California Division of Occupational Safety and Health (Cal-OSHA) Elevator, Ride & Tramway unit regulates rides and devices at large theme parks, smaller parks, fairs, traveling carnivals, and places offering bungees (see the next chapter for more on bungee jumping) or waterslides. Dry slides are explicitly exempt from regulation. Inflatables, whether they are located at a traveling carnival or permanent amusement park, or are rented from a private business, do not meet the definition of amusement ride under California law and therefore are not regulated by the state, but are regulated by the federal CPSC.

For permanent park rides, state inspectors perform an annual records audit, unannounced operational inspections, and physical inspection of the ride each year. In addition, ride owners are required to have a Qualified Safety Inspector certify annually that each ride meets industry standards and state regulations.

All portable amusement rides are inspected before they are originally put into operation for the public's use and at least once every year thereafter. Additionally, portable rides may be inspected each time they are disassembled and reassembled. Cal-OSHA regulations require all ride owners to report accidents resulting in death or injuries requiring medical attention other than ordinary first aid. As of 2008, portable ride owners must report major mechanical failures and any accident in which a patron falls or is ejected from the ride mid-cycle, regardless of injury.

California law requires the owner/operator of an amusement ride to be familiar with the ride manufacturer's information on assembling and maintaining an amusement ride and follow the manufacturer's recommendations, service bulletins, warnings of defective conditions, recalls, etc. Of course, the ride-owner/operator's failure to read and follow all of the manufacturer's instructions and warnings regarding the assembly, construction, operation, maintenance, and take-down of an amusement or recreational ride can lead to an injury to or death of riders and provide a basis of carelessness ("negligence") on the part of the ride's owner or operator.

AMUSEMENT RIDES AS "COMMON CARRIERS"

In one case, a 23-year-old woman suffered a severe brain injury and eventually died from her injuries several weeks after riding on the Indiana Jones amusement ride at Disneyland in Anaheim. The deceased woman's estate sued Disneyland, claiming that the woman had suffered serious brain injuries due to the violent shaking and stresses imposed by the ride. The estate alleged that the Indiana Jones attraction utilized jeep-style ride vehicles that were computer-controlled with 160,000 different combinations.

The estate alleged that the ride was "fast, turbulent, combining the ups and downs of a roller coaster with jarring jumps, drops, and unpredictable movements," and that the Indiana Jones attraction shook and whipsawed riders "with such fury that many passengers are forced to seek first aid and in some instances hospitalization."

The woman's estate claimed that the ride's sudden changes in direction could and did cause bleeding in the woman's brain similar to what happens in "shaken-baby syndrome." The case was appealed to the California Supreme Court on the question of whether or not the amusement ride was a "common carrier." The reason for designating a ride as a common carrier goes to the duty of safety (standard of care) the owner/operator of the amusement ride owes its riders. If designated a "common carrier," the amusement ride owner/operator is held to a higher standard of care than would normally be applied (i.e., ordinary carelessness or negligence). Examples of common carriers are buses, trains, and subways that carry passengers for a fee.

The Supreme Court of California ruled that the Indiana Jones ride met the "common carrier" criteria, despite the fact that it started and ended in the same place and did not transport passengers from one site to another. The fact that a passenger begins and ends the ride in the same place does not mean that she has not been transported. As the California Supreme Court stated in one case, "A tourist in San Francisco who takes a round-trip ride on a cable car solely for entertainment has been transported and is no less entitled to a safe ride than another passenger on the same cable car who disembarks to visit a store or restaurant."

As a common carrier with regard to its rides, the amusement park, traveling ride owner/operator, or other ride owner/operator owes its riders the highest degree of care for their safety and is legally responsible ("liable") for all of the costs and expenses caused by even the slightest bit of carelessness ("negligence") of the ride's owner/operator. An amusement park or traveling carnival must use the utmost degree of care and diligence for the safe passage of its riders, must provide everything necessary for that purpose, and must exercise to that end a reasonable degree of skill. Owners and operators of amusement rides are legally required to do all that human care, vigilance, and foresight reasonably can do under the circumstances.

Owners and operators of amusement rides are liable to their riders for injuries or death if they were even the slightest bit careless ("negligent") in the operation, maintenance, design, construction, or warnings associated with the ride. Further, the owner or operator of an amusement ride is required to provide vehicles and rides that are safe and fit for the purposes to which they are put, and is not excused for default in this respect by any degree of care.

Roller coasters have been considered "common carriers" in California since at least 1934 when the California Supreme Court so ruled in a personal injury case. In that case, the court described the ride upon which the victim was injured as a "roller coaster" that was "in the nature of a miniature scenic railway consisting of a train of small cars constructed to carry two passengers each." The owner and operator of a scenic railway in an amusement park is subject, where he has accepted payment from passengers on such railway, to the liabilities of a carrier of passengers generally, i.e., a common carrier. The common carrier's higher standard of care originated in English common law, and is based on a recognition that the privilege of serving the public as a common carrier necessarily entails great responsibility, requiring common carriers to exercise a high duty of care toward their customers.

The common carrier rule that applies to amusement rides is not limited to roller coasters and high-speed thrill rides. In one case, the court held that the operators of a horse-drawn stagecoach ride at Disneyland were common carriers, and were therefore held to the higher standard of care when the horses became frightened and ran, causing the coach to tip over, injuring the riders. The common-carrier rule was also applied in a personal injury case arising out of the "Pirates of the Caribbean" amusement ride at Disneyland. Several riders were injured when the boat in which they were riding was struck from behind by another boat. The appellate court held that the boat ride came within California's broad definition of a "common carrier," as Disneyland offered to carry riders from the mass public and therefore owed the riders the duty of utmost care and diligence.

The operator of a mule train that took passengers from Palm Springs to Tahquitz Falls and back was considered a common carrier and therefore was held to a higher standard of care for protecting his customers from harm. Holding that the mule train was a common carrier, the court concluded: "The only reasonable conclusion to be drawn from these facts is that a person who paid a roundtrip fare for the purpose of being conducted by mule over the designated route between fixed termini, purchased a ride; that the [owner/operator] offered to carry such a person by mule along that route between these termini; and that the transaction between them constituted an agreement of carriage."

The owner and operator of an amusement ride, be it at a set permanent place, such as Disneyland, or a traveling ride such as the ones that follow county fairs across the state, is required to provide its riders with rides that are "safe and fit for the purposes to which they are put." This means that the ride and its cars must be in good working condition and are safe to carry riders. For instance, the owner/operator of the amusement or recreational ride owes its customers the duty to ensure that the brakes on the ride are in good working condition so that it will stop at the end of the ride without careening into other cars in front of it, that all cables are in good condition so that the cable pulling a car up a rise doesn't break, causing the car to travel back downward into another car, and that seatbelts and safety bars are working properly in general and are properly secured by the owner/operator or his employees when a rider sits in the car. The owner/ operator of an amusement ride also has the obligation to inspect the entire ride periodically to see if there are any cracks, failing welds, or other defects in the ride that could fail or break, causing injury to or death of the riders.

Amusement rides have inherent dangers due to speed and mechanical complexities. They are operated for profit and are held out to the public to be safe. They are operated in the expectation that thousands of visitors, many of them children, will occupy their seats. Riders of roller coasters and other thrill rides seek the illusion of danger while being assured of their actual safety. The rider expects to be surprised and perhaps even frightened, but not hurt. The rule that carriers of passengers are held to the highest degree of care is based on the recognition that "to his diligence and fidelity are entrusted the lives and safety of large numbers of human beings." The California Supreme Court has stated that this rule applies equally to all common carriers, be it an amusement park ride bus, airplane, train, or other form of transportation.

INFLATABLE SLIDES AND BOUNCY CASTLES

Each year, inflatable rides account for approximately 5,000 users being injured or killed nationwide. Inflatable slides and bouncy castles of the type one might find at a church fair or a private birthday party are not subject to the "common carrier" rule, as they do not transport the users. Nevertheless, the owner/operator of the inflatable attraction has the obligation to use reasonable care in ensuring the inflatable is safe for use and is required to maintain, erect, and operate the attraction in a reasonably safe condition to prevent users of the inflatable from an undue risk of harm.

For instance, if the inflatable is improperly erected and secured, or is old and worn, if it deflates causing a user to suffer injuries—such as broken bones or head or brain injuries—then the company that rented, erected, maintained, or operated the ride may be legally responsible ("liable") for the user's injuries or death. The owner/operator of the inflatable is required to give the renter of the inflatable complete instructions on the proper use of the inflatable and any warnings as to how it should not be used or weight limits to protect the users from undue harm.

If the owner/operator of the inflatable attraction fails to use due care in setting up the inflatable, making sure that it is properly secured to the ground so that is does not move around or can be blown over by the wind, and is properly inflated, she can be liable for all injuries and damage caused by her negligence. An inflatable castle or other "moon bounce" attraction must be securely anchored so that a gust of wind will not blow it over, causing injuries to or death of the users. Sometimes the inflatable will suddenly deflate, causing the users to fall hard to the ground, suffering broken limbs, internal injuries, traumatic brain injury, and even death.

WHAT TO DO IF YOU HAVE BEEN INJURED ON AN AMUSEMENT RIDE

If you have been injured on an amusement park ride, on a traveling carnival ride, or at a private birthday party or other event that rented defective rides and inflatables, you should seek medical attention as soon as possible. That dizziness or headache you feel after a thrill ride may be symptomatic of a traumatic brain injury that requires immediate treatment. Pain in the back or limbs should be evaluated as soon as possible at the nearest emergency department to ensure that no bones are broken. Be aware that if you injured your neck or back and cannot move your legs or arms, or have tingling in your hands or feet, you should not move or be moved but should rather call the paramedics right away and stay immobilized until they arrive. The paramedics will properly secure you to a hard spine or cervical board before transporting you to the hospital. If your spine is not immobilized properly before you are taken to the hospital, your spinal cord could be injured further resulting in serious injury, such as quadriplegia or paraplegia. (This type of injury is discussed in detail in Chapter 29.)

If you have been injured or a loved one killed in an amusement ride accident, you should contact an experienced personal injury lawyer as soon as possible. This gives the lawyer the chance to see the accident scene and check out the ride before the owner/operator has the chance to make any modifications to it. Hiring a lawyer immediately is especially important when you have been injured by an amusement ride at a traveling midway or carnival so the lawyer can send out his investigators before the ride has been dismantled and moved to another part of the state or country, resulting in the loss of key evidence.

24 RECREATIONAL AND SPECTATOR SPORTS

PARTICIPATION IN RECREATIONAL SPORTS

Suppose you're playing in a friendly game of pickup basketball at your local park. Another player misses a shot and you go for the ball on the rebound. However, a player on the opposing team goes after the ball, too. The other player starts flailing his arms and hits you in the eye with an elbow, causing you to become blind in that eye. Can you sue the other player for the lost vision in your eye and all that comes with it? Well, you can sue him but you won't win.

According to the California Supreme Court, careless conduct ("negligence") by other players is an inherent risk in many sports, and holding co-participants liable for resulting injuries or deaths would discourage vigorous competition. The California Supreme Court held that those involved in a sporting activity do not have a duty to reduce the risk of harm that is inherent in the sport itself. They do, however, have a duty not to increase that inherent risk through behavior that is intentional or is "so reckless as to be totally outside the range of the ordinary activity involved in the sport."

Whether a person assumes the risk of being injured depends on the nature of the sport or activity in question and the person's relationship to that activity. In the context of sports, the question turns on whether a given injury is within the "inherent risk of the sport." Conduct is totally outside the range of ordinary activity involved in the sport if the prohibition of that conduct would neither deter vigorous participation in the sport nor otherwise fundamentally alter the nature of the sport.

In a landmark case, a player carelessly knocked over a co-participant and stepped on her hand during a touch football game. The California Supreme Court ruled that the conduct was an inherent risk of the sport and therefore rejected the injured player's complaint for monetary damages on the basis that she had assumed the risk of being injured. The Court reasoned that vigorous participation in such sporting events likely would be chilled if legal liability were to be imposed on a participant on the basis of his ordinary careless conduct.

By choosing to participate in the sport, a person assumes that level of risk inherent in the sport. In a sports context, a court does not look at which risks a particular participant subjectively knew of and chose to encounter. Rather, the court evaluates the fundamental nature of the sport and the offending player's role in or relationship to that sport in order to determine whether the player owed a duty to protect a participant from the particular risk of harm.

The degree of the risk anticipated varies from sport to sport. While bodily harm is expected in prize fighting, the fighters do not consent to or assume the risk of being stabbed or shot in the ring. At the other extreme, in bridge or table tennis, bodily harm is not contemplated at all. As one court stated: "The correct rule is this: If the defendant's actions, even those which might cause incidental physical damage in some sports, are within the ordinary expectations of the participants—such as blocking in football, checking in hockey, knock-out punches in boxing, and aggressive riding in horse racing—no cause of action can succeed based on a resulting injury."

For example, in baseball, a batter is not supposed to carelessly throw the bat after getting a hit and starting to run to first base. However, the "assumption of risk" doctrine recognizes that "vigorous bat deployment" is an integral part of the sport of baseball and a risk players assume when they choose to participate. Especially in the heat of competition, and in an effort to get to first base quickly, a batter may be careless in getting rid of the bat. Under the assumption of risk doctrine, the hitter does not have a duty to other players or spectators to avoid carelessly throwing the bat after getting a hit.

A chilling effect on players participating in the sport would result from imposing liability on players for ordinary careless conduct. The California Supreme Court stated that "even when a participant's conduct violates a rule of the game and may subject the violator to internal sanctions prescribed by the sport itself, imposition of legal liability for such conduct might well alter fundamentally the nature of the sport by deterring participants from vigorously engaging in activity." Accordingly, the California Supreme Court has held that co-participants' limited duty of care is to refrain from intentionally injuring one another or engaging in conduct that is so reckless as to be totally outside the range of the ordinary activity involved in the sport.

It doesn't make a difference if one of the participants is penalized for such actions by the officials. Routine rule violations, such as clipping in football, low blows in boxing, and fouls in horse races are common occurrences and within the scope of the athletes' expectations. In an intercollegiate baseball game, a pitcher on the Rio Hondo Community College team hit a batter on the Citrus Community College team with a normal pitch. The next inning, the Citrus pitcher allegedly retaliated by hitting a Rio Hondo batter with a "beanball." The Rio Hondo player sued the Citrus Community College District for negligence. The California Supreme Court ruled that the suit was barred by the assumption of risk doctrine, stating that while it is against the rules of baseball to intentionally throw at a batter, being intentionally thrown at is a fundamental part and inherent risk of the sport of baseball. The Court commented that it is not the function of personal injury ("tort") law to police such conduct.

As for non-contact sports such as golf, the California Supreme Court held that the "assumption of risk" doctrine applies and that being struck by a carelessly hit golf ball is an inherent risk of the sport. In determining whether the defendant acted recklessly, the trier of fact (i.e., the jury) must consider both the nature of the game and the totality of circumstances surrounding the shot. In making a golf shot, the player focuses on the ball, unlike other sports in which a player's focus is divided between the ball and other players. That is not to say that a golfer may ignore other players before making a shot.

Ordinarily, a golfer should not make a shot without checking to see whether others are reasonably likely to be struck. Once having addressed the ball, a golfer is not required to break his concentration by checking the field again. Nor must a golfer conduct a head count of the other players in the group before making a shot. Many factors will bear on whether a golfer's conduct was reasonable, negligent, or reckless. Relevant circumstances may include: (1) the golfer's skill level, (2) whether topographical undulations, trees, or other impediments obscured his view, (3) what steps he took to determine whether anyone was within range, and (4) the distance and angle between a plaintiff and defendant.

In one case, a student rock climber was killed after a fall allegedly caused by his instructors' improper placement of rope anchors. The court rejected the survivors' lawsuit, stating that "Falling, whether because of one's own slip, a co-climber's stumble, or an anchor system giving way, is the very risk inherent in the sport of mountain climbing and cannot be completely eliminated without destroying the sport itself." That court further found that the defendant met the burden of proving that the climber was not taken beyond his level of experience and capability in the activity culminating in his fall, and that the risk to him was not beyond that inherent in any climbing activity.

A sport instructor may be found to have breached a duty of care to a student or athlete only if the instructor intentionally injures the student or engages in conduct that is reckless in the sense that it is totally outside the range of the ordinary activity involved in teaching or coaching the sport. A 14-year-old novice on a school swim team broke her neck during a meet when she executed a practice dive into a shallow racing pool located on school property. The California Supreme Court held that the case should go to trial as a jury could find that the coach's conduct was reckless in that it fell totally outside the range of ordinary activity involved in teaching or coaching the sport.

The injured girl presented evidence of the coach's failure to provide her with training in shallow-water diving, his awareness of the girl's intense fear of diving into shallow water, his conduct in lulling the girl into a false sense of security by promising that she would not be required to dive at competitions, his last-minute breach of this promise in the heat of competition, and his threat to remove her from competition or at least from the meet if she refused to dive. The girl's evidence also supported the conclusion that the maneuver of diving into a shallow racing pool, if not done correctly, posed a significant risk of extremely serious injury, and that there is a well-established mode of instruction for teaching a student to perform this maneuver safely. The court found that the evidence presented by the injured girl raised a disputed issue of fact as to whether the coach provided any instruction at all to the girl with regard to the safe performance of such a dive, as well as to the existence and nature of the coach's promises and threats. Thus, the court concluded the girl was entitled to a trial in front of a fair and impartial jury and her lawsuit should not be thrown out.

In the context of snow skiing, the courts have held that the participant assumes the risk of being injured by moguls on a ski run, snow-covered stumps, variations in terrain, changes in surface or subsurface snow conditions, bare spots, other skiers, snow-making equipment, and many other hazards which must be considered inherent in the sport of skiing. Generally, a skier is not liable for running into another skier, because it is not done recklessly or deliberately, but is usually the result of mere ordinary carelessness (negligence). However, while inadvertent collisions are an inherent risk of skiing and therefore assumed by the participants, a skier does not assume the risk that other skiers will ski while intoxicated. The increased risks of injury created by the consumption of alcohol are not inherent in the sport of skiing.

However, not all risks of being injured while using the slopes are assumed. For instance, a skier who was struck and injured by a runaway snowboard that was not equipped with a retention strap was not barred from suing the careless snowboarder. The court held that the assumption of risk doctrine was not an absolute bar to recovery on the facts presented, as the jury could find that the lack of a retention strap increased the risk of harm to the victim beyond what was inherent in the sport of skiing.

Although a snow skier or snowboarder assumes the risks inherent in the activity, that does not include assuming the risk that he may be injured by a defective chair lift. A snow skier or snowboarder puts his life and limbs in the hands of the owner or operator of a chair lift, gondola, or tram that takes people up to the top of the mountain. In California, a chair lift or tram is deemed to be a "common carrier" of skiers and others up (or down) the hill. As such, it owes its riders the duty of utmost care and diligence. A cable car company that, for a fee, shuttles passengers up the snowless slopes of a mountain for downhill bike riders, sightseeing, and other activities is a common carrier, too.

A commercial operator of a horse-riding facility has the duty to supply horses that are not unduly dangerous, to warn patrons renting a given horse of its predisposition to behave in certain ways which add to the ordinary risk of horse riding, to not provide faulty saddles, and to not provide dangerous trails. Being cut by the blade of another skater during a group figure skating session is an inherent risk of the sport, and the injured skater cannot recover for personal injuries under the doctrine of "primary assumption of risk."

Bungee jumping is a popular pastime for many people who want to feel the experience of flying and the freedom it brings. Unfortunately, sometimes the bungee cord is not secured properly, or otherwise fails to stop the rider's fall, causing the rider to free-fall a total of hundreds of feet, resulting in serious injuries, even death. Owners and operators of bungee jumping companies must check the bungee cord regularly to ensure that it is still safe and sound. The person who is actually securing the bungee cord to the stationary surface—such as a bridge—must make sure that the bungee cord is properly fastened and will not slip or break when the person stretches the bungee cord to the limit, putting the most pressure on the site where the bungee cord is secured.

The operator must also make sure that the bungee cord and equipment are property fastened to the jumper's leg and foot, ensuring that it will not break or the jumper's leg will not come out of the equipment. Often, a person who participates in a bungee jump is given a "written release of liability" or waiver to sign, in which she promises not to sue the bungee-jumping company if she is injured in the jump, even if the injury is due to some carelessness (negligence) on the bungee-jumping company's part. Such releases of liability, sometimes called a waiver, are discussed below.

NEGLIGENT DESIGN OF COURSE

Although a person may be barred from recovery on the basis that he assumed the risks inherent in the sport, one risk that is not assumed is that the playing field or course has been negligently designed, thereby increasing the risk of harm to the participant beyond what is inherent in the sport. This was the case in a lawsuit that involved a 17-year-old boy who was injured while racing his bicycle on the defendant's bicycle motocross (BMX) course. By its nature, BMX racing includes bumps, jumps, turns, straight-aways and obstacles. The boy was injured on the "million dollar jump," which consisted of two bumps joined together in a saddle-like configuration.

Both parties (the victim and the BMX operator) submitted declarations of experts that conflicted on the cause of the injury. The injured boy's expert stated that the "million dollar jump" was defectively designed in that the slope of the first hill of the jump was too steep and caused the rider's center of gravity to rise too abruptly, leading to the accident. The BMX operator's expert witness submitted a declaration in which he stated that the jumps at the BMX park were of the type that could be expected at any BMX track. The court held that there is a duty to refrain from using BMX jumps that by design pose an extreme risk of injury, and it was a question of fact for the jury to decide whether that duty was breached by virtue of the design of the million dollar jump.

The court stated that it is not unreasonable to expect a BMX course to refrain from utilizing jumps that by design create an extreme risk of injury. Certainly the jumps and falls are inherent to the sport, and there is no duty to eliminate the jumps entirely. Nor is there a duty to protect a participant from injury arising from reasonably designed jumps. However, the sport does not inherently require jumps that are designed in such a way as to create an extreme risk of injury. The court concluded that a duty to exercise due care is owed to a bicycle racer injured on a bicycle jump that by its design creates an extreme risk of injury.

Likewise, a golfer assumes the risk that she may be hit by an errant golf ball; however, she doesn't assume the risk that the golf course has been negligently designed in such a way that increases the risk of being injured beyond what is reasonably expected.

EXPRESS RELEASES OF LIABILITY

Before you are allowed to participate in a recreational activity— be it rock climbing, horse riding, participating in a baseball league, a bicycle race, a running marathon, bungee jumping, or parachuting, for example—you may be asked to sign a written "express release of liability" (also known as a "hold harmless" contract, a waiver agreement, or an exculpatory clause). An express release of liability is an assumption of risk by which you, in advance, take your chances of injury from known (and sometimes unknown) risks arising from what the other party is to do or leaves undone. A well-drafted release relieves the other party of his legal duty to you; that is, he cannot be held liable to you even if he was careless ("negligent"). However, a release that does not clearly and unambiguously inform an ordinary person untrained in the law that its purpose and effect is to relieve the owner/operator of the business of responsibility is not enforceable and will not bar a lawsuit by a person who was injured by the other party's negligence.

A release—no matter how well written—cannot relieve the party from wrongdoing more serious than negligence, such as gross negligence, recklessness and intentional misconduct. The release agreement is usually given on a take-it-or-leave-it-basis, and you have no negotiating or bargaining power; the release is valid unless it involves the "public interest." However,

California courts have uniformly refused to find a public interest or to invalidate releases from liability for ordinary negligence for injuries that occur in the context and course of sports and recreational activities.

Just because you may have signed a release or received a pass or ticket with a waiver or release written on it does not necessarily mean that you are out of luck. To be effective to relieve a party from future carelessness or misconduct, the release must be clear, explicit, and comprehensible in each of its essential details. If the language is ambiguous or convoluted so that it does not clearly notify you that you cannot sue the party even if he was negligent, the release is invalid. If the release is printed in fine print on a portion of a document you are not likely to notice, the release may not apply. Under contract law, if there is any ambiguity about the meaning of a word, phrase, sentence, or entire paragraph, it is construed against the party that drafted the release.

A release that was both broad and explicit and through which a rock climber not only expressly acknowledged and assumed "all the risks" of rock climbing activities, both known and unknown, "whether caused or alleged to be caused by the negligent acts or omissions" of the rock climbing facility was enforceable and provided a complete defense to the lawsuit filed by a seasoned rock climber who was injured in a fall.

INJURIES TO SPECTATORS AT SPORTING EVENTS

Foul balls hit into the spectators' area clearly create a risk of injury at baseball games. But if such foul balls were to be eliminated, it would be impossible to play the game. Thus, the risk of being hit by a foul ball is an inherent risk to spectators attending baseball games. The owner of a baseball stadium has no duty to protect spectators from the natural hazards generated by the way in which the game itself is played. In determining whether an individual should be compensated for her injury and in crafting a rule that would permit or reject such compensation, there is a group of persons other than the immediate parties whose interests are worthy of consideration. Those are the literally millions of people who attend baseball games all over the country.

In one lawsuit by a spectator who was hit by a foul ball, the court stated,

As we see it, to permit plaintiff to recover under the circumstances here would force baseball stadiums to do one of two things: (1) place all spectator areas behind a protective screen thereby reducing the quality of everyone's view, and since players are often able to reach into the spectator area to catch foul balls, changing the very nature of the game itself; or (2) continue the status quo and increase the price of tickets to cover the cost of compensating injured persons with the attendant result that persons of meager means might be "priced out" of enjoying the great American pastime. To us, neither alternative is acceptable. In our opinion it is not the role of the court to effect a wholesale remodeling of a revered American institution through application of [personal injury] law.

One of the natural risks assumed by spectators attending professional baseball games is that of being struck by batted or thrown balls. The management is not required, nor does it undertake, to insure patrons against injury from such sources. All that is required is the exercise of ordinary care to protect patrons against such injuries and, in doing so, the management is not obliged to screen all seats, because many patrons prefer to sit where their view is not obscured by a screen. Moreover, the management is not required to provide screened seats for all who may apply for them. The duty imposed by the law is performed when screened seats are provided for as many as may be reasonably expected to ask for them on any ordinary occasion.

If a spectator chooses to occupy an unscreened seat or is unable to obtain a secured seat and consequently occupies one that is not protected, she is considered to be sufficiently warned of the risk of being hit by a foul ball or a thrown or broken bat by common knowledge of the sport, and assumes the risk of being struck by thrown or batted balls. If such a spectator is injured thereby, she is therefor barred from recovering damages. The courts reason that a person who fears being injured always has the option of not attending a baseball game or sitting in a part of the park that is out of reach of balls traveling with enough speed to cause them harm.

One woman who was an ardent Los Angeles Dodgers fan was injured when she was struck in the head by a foul ball and filed a lawsuit to recover the costs and expenses of her injuries and other damages. The court held that the woman had impliedly consented to take her own chances that she would not be injured by voluntarily electing to sit in a seat that was clearly unprotected by any form of screening. The court stated that, rather than request a seat in a section where injury was unlikely to occur, the woman chose to accept a highly sought after seat, close to the "sphere of action," where the likelihood of foul balls entering the stands remained a possibility. She was sufficiently warned of the risk by the common knowledge of the nature of the sport and by the warning provided on the back of her ticket. Thus, the court concluded that the Dodgers were under no duty to do anything further to protect her from that hazard.

However, not all risks of being hit by a foul ball are necessarily assumed by the spectators. A spectator at a minor league professional baseball game was sitting in an uncovered section of the stadium when a foul ball struck him in the face.

Immediately before being hit, the team's mascot (a man dressed in a dinosaur costume as a character named "Tremor") was behind the victim and the mascot's tail was hitting the victim on the head and shoulders. The victim turned to see what the mascot was doing, and as he was turning back around to face the field, a foul ball hit him before he could react to it. The court agreed with the general rule that the risk of being hit with a foul ball was inherent in the sport of baseball and such risk was therefore assumed by spectators.

However, the court found that in this case the antics of the mascot may have increased the inherent risk to the victim and was a question of fact for the jury to decide at a trial. The court noted that the antics of a mascot were not an essential or integral part of the playing of a baseball game, and the game could be played in the absence of such antics. Indeed, the person who dressed up as the mascot submitted a sworn written statement (a "declaration") that there were occasional games when he had not been there, but the game was nevertheless played.

Of course, if a person chooses to sit in a seat that is protected by a screen, but the screen turns out to be defective and lets a foul ball through to hit and injure the spectator, the spectator may have the right to sue the owner/operator of the stadium for her injuries.

The rule against spectators being hit by flying debris does not apply solely to baseball stadiums. A woman was injured when, during pre-game warm-ups at a Los Angeles Kings ice hockey game, a puck flew off the ice and struck her in the mouth. The woman claimed that the "assumption of risk" doctrine did not apply in her case. She asserted that while the risk of being hit by a puck at an ice hockey game is an assumed risk, the risk of having her view blocked by large groups of spectators congregating near the ice so she could not see the playing surface or the puck was not an inherent risk of the game. The court denied her claim, stating that just as baseball stadium owners owe no duty to eliminate the risk of injury from foul balls, the owner of an ice rink owes no duty to eliminate the inherent risk of injury from flying pucks during a hockey game or warm-ups.

As for the injured spectator's contention that she did not assume the risk that her view would be blocked by groups of people milling around in front of her, the court held that obstructions of view caused by the unpredictable movements of other fans are an inherent and unavoidable part of attending a sporting event. The court noted that views are blocked whenever fans spontaneously leap to their feet or move to and from their seats.

25 AVIATION LAW

Aircraft accidents—whether involving a four-seat private small plane or a commercial jumbo jet—can present difficult questions of fact and law regarding whether the owner and/or operator of the plane is legally responsible ("liable") for injuries or death arising from his carelessness or the carelessness of his employees. And even if the owner or operator of the aircraft is liable for the injuries, there may be laws that limit the amount of money the injured passenger or the survivors of a passenger who was killed can recover.

PRIVATE AIRPLANES

Hundreds of thousands of Americans own small aircraft that they use for pleasure flying, attending fly-ins with airplane clubs, and taking vacations, among other things. Suppose your friend owns a small plane and asks you if you'd like to go for a ride. You enthusiastically agree. However, while in mid-flight, there is a problem with the engine and it stops the propeller from turning, and you crash land. Can you sue your friend for injuries you suffered in the crash? Or in the case of fatal injuries, can your loved ones sue your friend's estate for your "wrongful death?"

A privately-owned noncommercial plane owner does not

regularly charge a fee for transporting persons—whether the flight is just for a couple of hours of sightseeing or your friend is taking you from one place to another—and so she is considered a "private carrier." As such, your friend has the legal obligation ("owes you a duty") to use ordinary and due care in making sure the plane is airworthy and that she is qualified and fit to be at the controls and not make any careless errors that would result in the passenger's harm or death. In legalese, the "standard of care" applicable to private pilots flying pleasure craft is one of "ordinary care" for the safe transportation of their passengers. Ordinary care is that degree of care that an ordinarily prudent person would use under like circumstances when charged with a like duty. Ordinary negligence is a lack of due care; and due care means commensurate care, under the circumstances, tested by the standard of reasonable prudence and foresight.

The pilot of the small plane must perform a careful and thorough pre-flight inspection of the plane to ensure that it is indeed safe to fly, i.e., airworthy. She must also be familiar with the weather conditions on the route to your destination. If the pilot is qualified to fly only under visual flight rules (VFR), she must avoid flying into a storm, fog, or other inclement weather that requires an instrument flight rating and the appropriate instruments, indicators, and gauges in the plane to allow her to fly under instrument flight rules (IFR).

Because small planes are not required to have cockpit recording devices or flight data recorders, it may be more difficult to pinpoint the cause of a small plane's crash than the crash of a commercial airliner. However, the National Transportation and Safety Board (NTSB) has jurisdiction over the investigation of accidents involving planes of all sizes, and can often determine the cause of the accident.

COMMERCIAL FLIGHTS

Commercial aviation involves transport "for compensation or hire." This includes airlines, commuter airplanes, and charter aircraft, but does not include corporate aircraft or privately owned airplanes. Commercial flying is considered to be one of the safest—if not indeed the safest—means of transportation going. You have a much greater chance of being injured in an automobile accident on your way to the airport than you do of being involved in a commercial aircraft accident. Unfortunately, when there is a commercial aircraft accident, it tends to be a major disaster resulting in tens, even hundreds of injuries and deaths and significant property damage.

When a commercial aircraft is involved in an accident that results in loss of life or serious personal injuries, there may be a number of possible defendants who may be legally responsible ("liable") for the injuries or death. First there is the airline company itself. Because commercial airliners offer to the general public to carry goods or persons and are bound to accept anyone who offers to pay the "price of carriage" depending on seat availability, they are considered by law to be "common carriers."

As a common carrier, an air carrier and its employees are required to use the "utmost due care and diligence" for the safe passage of, and to prevent injuries to, its passengers, and it can be held financially responsible for injuries resulting from even its slightest carelessness ("negligence"). Commercial airlines are bound to do all that, which with human care, vigilance, and foresight, they can reasonably do under the circumstances to protect their passengers from harm. "Passengers" include not only persons who are on board the aircraft when it crashes, but also passengers who are injured or killed while getting on ("embarking") or off ("disembarking") the plane. However, as to other planes and persons who are not passengers, the airliner owes them only the ordinary standard of care, that is, the duty not to expose them to an unnecessary risk of harm (ordinary negligence).

A common carrier is one who holds itself out to the public as engaged in the public business of transporting persons for compensation from place to place, offering its services to those members of the public generally who choose to employ it and pay its charges. The distinctive characteristic of a common carrier is that it undertakes to hold itself out to the public, either expressly or as a course of conduct, as a business to carry for hire on a uniform tariff all persons wanting transportation, so long as it has the room to accommodate them.

"Holding oneself out to the public" means that the carrier in some way makes it known to its prospective patrons the fact that its services are available. This may be done in various ways, as by advertising, solicitation, or the establishment in a community of a known place of business where requests for service will be received. However the result may be accomplished, the essential thing is that there must be a public offering of the service, or, in other words, a communication of the fact that service is available to those who may wish to use it.

For a transporter of passengers such as an airplane to be a common carrier, it is not necessary that it have a regular schedule of flights, a fixed route, or a relatively unlimited carrying capacity. For example, a carrier that provides air transportation may limit its operations solely to charter flights and still be legally considered to be a common carrier. Important factors used to determine whether an operation is a common carrier include an established place of business, engaging in the operation as a regular business and not merely as a casual or occasional undertaking, and a regular schedule of charges.

To be a common carrier, it is not necessary for the carrier to leave one place and transport its passengers to another place. A sightseeing tour that embarks from and returns to the same point can be considered a common carrier. Hence, an airplane pilot who offered sightseeing flights to the ocean and back was held to be a common carrier, even though the flights took off and landed at the same airport. Similarly, a company that provides sightseeing helicopter rides for a fee is a common carrier, even though it takes off and lands at the same helipad. Commercial hot air balloons that advertise or otherwise promote their business of sightseeing trips from Point A to Point B are also considered common carriers.

Although common carriers must use the utmost care and diligence for their passengers' safe carriage, must provide everything necessary for that purpose, and must exercise to that end a reasonable degree of skill, a common carrier is not an insurer of its passengers' safety, and does not give them an absolute guarantee that nothing will go wrong and they will not be injured or killed in any way whatsoever.

The airline, as a common carrier, is also legally required to provide vehicles (in this case, aircraft) that are safe and fit for the purpose to which they are put, and is not excused for default in this respect by any degree of care. Also, the passenger's motive for seeking transportation is not relevant in determining the carrier's liability. The common carrier owes the same high duty of utmost care whether the passenger rides for pleasure or business. A passenger's purpose in purchasing transportation, whether it be to get from one place to another or to travel simply for pleasure or sightseeing, does not determine whether the provider of the transportation is a carrier for reward. Undisclosed purposes on the passengers' part do not affect the duty of the common carrier to exercise the highest degree of care for the safety of the passenger.

The major causes of a commercial aircraft accident are:

- Pilot error
- Mechanical failure due to faulty equipment

- Bad weather
- Failing to properly de-ice the plane before take-off
- Air traffic controller error
- Improper maintenance or repair of the aircraft or its component parts
- Violating Federal Aviation Administration (FAA) regulations
- Structural or design problems with the aircraft
- Sabotage (bombs, hijacking, shoot-downs)

Other causes include improper loading of the aircraft and fuel contamination.

The airline company may be held responsible for the errors of its pilots in operating the aircraft, its maintenance crew for failing to maintain the aircraft properly or failing to detect a crack or other structural problem with the aircraft, or its employees for improperly loading or over-loading the aircraft. The manufacturer of the aircraft or supplier of a component part may be held liable under the doctrine of "strict product liability" (discussed in Chapter 21, "Defective Products") for any and all defects in the manufacture or design of the plane or its defective parts that caused or contributed to the accident. Similarly, the United States government may be liable where the accident is due to the negligence of one or more of its employees, usually the air traffic controllers. In a collision with another aircraft, the other aircraft may be sued if its pilots were negligent in failing to avoid the crash.

An all-too-frequent yet completely preventable cause of injuries and deaths in aircraft accidents involve "runway incursions." The FAA defines a runway incursion as "any occurrence at an airport involving an aircraft, vehicle, person, or object on the ground that creates a collision hazard or results in loss of separation with an aircraft taking off, intending to take off, landing, or intending to land." Runway incursions are frequently the result of the carelessness ("negligence") of air traffic controllers in managing the flow of air traffic on the ground.

Research has shown that the first three minutes of a flight and the last eight are when about 80 percent of airplane accidents take place. This is often referred to as the rule of "Plus Three/Minus Eight."

A professor in England analyzed the seating charts of more than a hundred plane crashes and interviewed 1,900 survivors and 155 cabin-crew members. He found that the people most likely to survive a plane crash are those sitting right next to the exit row or one row away. He discovered that survivors usually move an average of five rows before they can get off a burning aircraft. The professor's study concluded that beyond a five-row cutoff from the exit, your chances of surviving an aircraft fire are greatly reduced.

The National Transportation Safety Board (NTSB) is the governmental agency vested by Congress with the power to investigate all civilian aircraft accidents, whether it be a major airline disaster involving hundreds of deaths or a small, single-engine plane that goes down. Since its creation in 1967, the NTSB has investigated over 115,000 civilian aircraft accidents. After it has made a thorough investigation of the accident, the NTSB releases its report identifying the cause(s) of the crash—if a cause can be determined—and issues safety recommendations designed to prevent future accidents from the same cause.

In conducting its investigation, the NTSB gathers data from the plane's cockpit voice recorder and flight data recorder if the aircraft was equipped with them. In major air disasters, the NTSB attempts to piece together the remaining parts of the plane in a hangar or other facility to try to reconstruct the plane and find the cause of the accident. The Federal Aviation Administration (FAA) usually also takes part in the investigation to determine what accident prevention steps it should implement to prevent another occurrence of the same cause. The FAA provides the NTSB with technical advice about the aircraft and flight conditions as well.

Commuter planes and regional jets are generally mid-sized planes that connect smaller cities with large ones having major airports. On February 12, 2009, during Continental Connection Flight 3407, a flight operated by Colgan Air under contract to Continental, a commuter turboprop crashed into a home outside Buffalo, New York, killing 50 people—45 passengers, four crew members, and one person on the ground in the house. The plane involved was a Bombardier Dash 8 Q400, a 74-seat twin-engine, medium-range turboprop airliner. The plane was less than one year old and had flown for only about 1,500 hours.

Early speculation was that a buildup of ice on the wings was the most probable cause of the tragedy. However, approximately a month and a half after the disaster, the NTSB investigators stated that ice was not the likely cause of the crash and that it was looking at the actions of the pilot immediately before the crash. It was reported that the Flight Data Recorder indicated that the pilot's control column—basically, the device used to steer the plane—moved sharply backward, pitching the nose of the turboprop upward, causing the aircraft to stall. It is hard to recover from a stall like this, and the crew had only 1,600 to 1,800 feet to do so before the plane hit the ground. This was the deadliest American disaster in more than five years.

A fairly recent crash involving a commuter aircraft happened in the early morning hours of August 27, 2006. During Comair Flight 191, marketed as Delta Connection Flight 5191, a 50-seat Bombardier Canadair Regional Jet CRJ-100ER bound for Atlanta crashed while trying to take off from Blue Grass Airport in Fayette County, Kentucky, four miles west of Lexington. Forty-nine of the 50 occupants of the plane perished in the crash, with only the first officer (the copilot) surviving the crash.

In the Comair disaster, Flight 5191 was cleared for take-off on Runway 22. However, for some reason, the aircraft attempted to take off on Runway 26, a much shorter runway. The aircraft ran off the end of the runway, crashed through the airport perimeter fence, and came to rest in trees on an adjacent horse farm. The aircraft was destroyed by impact forces and a post-crash fire. The NTSB determined that the probable cause of the disaster was the flight crew's failure to use available cues and aids to identify the aircraft's location on the airport surface during taxi, as well as their failure to cross-check and verify that the aircraft was on the correct runway before take-off. Contributing factors were the flight crew's non-pertinent conversations during taxi, which resulted in a loss of positional awareness and the FAA's failure to require that all runway crossings be authorized only by specific air traffic control clearances.

In 1993, a commercial jet at Blue Grass Airport was cleared for take-off on Runway 22 but mistakenly went to the shorter Runway 26 instead. Fortunately, tower personnel noticed the mistake and cancelled the aircraft's take-off clearance just as the crew realized their error. The aircraft subsequently made a safe departure from Runway 22. On September 1, 2006, the FAA issued a Safety Alert for Operators (SAFO), titled "Flight Crew Techniques and Procedures that Enhance Pre-takeoff and Takeoff Safety." This alert highlights existing FAA aircraft ground operation guidance and reminds flight crews that maximum attention should be placed upon maintaining "situational awareness" during taxi operations.

DOMESTIC FLIGHTS

A domestic flight is one occurring entirely within the United States, with no stopovers in another country, whether for refueling or to let off or take on passengers. Unlike crashes involving international flights, passengers on domestic flights do not face any limitations on the amount of recovery the passengers can receive for their injuries or the survivors can receive for the death of their loved ones. Additionally, an injured passenger on a domestic flight can recover damages for purely emotional and mental injuries without having to prove any accompanying bodily injury, as she must do to recover such damages on an international flight.

When a passenger on a domestic commercial flight is killed in a crash, it may be possible for her next of kin to bring a "survival" action to recover monetary damages for the pain, suffering, and mental anguish the passenger experienced from the time she realized that something was seriously wrong with the flight until the time of her death.

When a commercial aircraft crashes, causing a loss of life or serious injuries, the air carrier and its insurance company will usually contact the injured passenger or next of kin right away and provide immediate medical or grief support. The airliner will often pay for the hotel costs of a deceased passenger's next of kin and help make and pay for funeral arrangements. The air carrier's representative or its insurance company's agent will frequently tell the survivors that there is no need for them to obtain a lawyer to represent them, as they will do right by them.

The insurance company may offer to pay what appears to the family to be a fair settlement. Do not accept any settlement offer from an insurance company without the advice of a skilled and experienced aviation accident lawyer. A grieving family is susceptible to accepting a much lower offer than an experienced aviation lawyer can get for them. Although the airliner or its insurance company will try to dissuade you from getting a lawyer saying that a lawyer's fee will come out of your share, the truth is that studies consistently show that victims of accidents end up with more money in their pockets even after paying the lawyer his fee.

An experienced personal injury law firm can also help with

seeing to it that you obtain appropriate and thorough medical care for your physical, emotional, and psychological injuries suffered as a result of the accident. They can also do everything possible to ensure that you obtain full compensation for your medical expenses, pain and suffering, mental anguish, property damage, lost wages, psychological injuries, loss of society, affection, and comfort, and all of your other injuries and damages.

INTERNATIONAL FLIGHTS

If you are injured or a loved one killed in an international flight, your rights are much more complicated than if you or your loved one were flying on a domestic flight. Up until 1997, the maximum recovery for damages due to injuries to or death of a passenger on an international flight was $75,000. This limit came from a series of treaties and agreements between airline companies and was known as the "Warsaw System."

In 1929, a treaty was formed in Warsaw, Poland that was intended to protect the new air industry from having to pay excessive damages in the event of an accident. Under its terms, the maximum amount an injured passenger or the family of a deceased passenger could recover was 125,000 francs (about $8,300 in U.S. currency at the time), unless the injury or death was caused by the "willful misconduct" of the airline or its employees, something that was extremely difficult to prove. According to the terms of the Warsaw Convention, an air carrier could escape liability by proving that it took "all necessary measures to avoid the damages or it was impossible for him or them to take such measures."

In return for the limitation on the amount of money the air carrier would have to pay to compensate injured passengers or families of deceased passengers, the Warsaw Convention created a basis of liability (a "cause of action") and established a presumption of air carrier liability for passenger death or bodily injury resulting from an accident occurring while the passenger was on board the aircraft or was in the process of embarking or disembarking the aircraft.

In 1955, the Hague Protocol increased the limit of liability to approximately $20,000. Then in 1966, in what is known as The Montreal Agreement, international air carriers agreed to enter into a "special contract" with passengers, giving them higher limitations on liability on international flights originating, terminating, or having a connection point in the United States. As a result of the Montreal Agreement, the damage amount on such international flights was raised to $75,000. The air carriers also agreed not to invoke the defense of having taken "all necessary measures," and they agreed as well that the $75,000 limitation would not apply if the airline or an employee engaged in willful misconduct that injured or resulted in the death of a passenger.

The Warsaw System led to some unfair results. Suppose two women were sitting side-by-side in an airliner. The plane was traveling from Los Angeles to London with a stopover in Bangor, Maine. One of the women planned on getting off the plane in Bangor; that was the end of her trip. The other woman intended to fly all the way to London. Now suppose that due to mechanical problems, the plane crashes while flying over the United States, killing all on board. For the woman who planned to end her trip at Bangor, Maine, her survivors could bring a wrongful death case against the airline with no limits on the amount of money her survivors could recover. However, for the passenger who intended to continue on the flight to London, the most her survivors could recover under the Warsaw System was $75,000.

In 1996, some 30 years after the Montreal Agreement, at the urging of the United States, many international air carriers considered whether their liability limits were too low. Finding that to be the case, a number of international air carriers, through the International Air Transport Association (IATA) and in cooperation with the United States Department of Transportation, signed a series of agreements designed to change the limits of liability for injured or killed passengers. Over 120 airlines signed the agreement, which removed the $75,000 limit of liability and allows passengers to recover full compensatory damages for physical injury or death in an "accident," according to the laws of the passenger's "domicile," which is usually the permanent place of his residence. The IATA Intercarrier Agreement provides that the international air carrier must pay up to 100,000 Special Drawing Rights (SDRs) to each injured passenger or the survivors of a deceased passenger without raising any defenses. (Special Drawing Rights are a mix of currency values established by the International Monetary Fund, and on June 1, 2009, the exchange rate was 1 SDR = 1.548 U.S. dollars.) This is a form of strict or absolute liability, in that the victims need not prove the air carrier was careless or negligent in any way to recover up to 100,000 SDRs. (approximately $154,800.00 U.S. currency). The international air carriers voluntarily waived the Warsaw System limits of liability for passenger injury and death, and allowed victims to make a claim for damages equal to what they could make if it had been a domestic flight. However, the Montreal Agreement continued the prohibition against recovering damages for emotional injuries and mental distress and anguish without some type of physical injury. It also continued the rule barring the recovery of punitive damages from the air carrier.

Then, in 1999, came The Montreal Convention for the Unification of Certain Rules for International Carriage by Air. The Montreal Convention is the new uniform and exclusive recovery method for applicable recoveries and purports to replace the entire patchwork Warsaw System. The Montreal Convention applies to all "international carriage" of persons, baggage, or cargo performed by aircraft for reward. It applies equally to gratuitous carriage by aircraft performed by an air transport undertaking.

Paragraph 1 of Article 17 of the Montreal Convention states that "[t]he carrier is liable for damages sustained in the case of death or bodily injury of a passenger upon condition only that the accident which caused the death or injury took place on board the aircraft or in the course of any of the operations of embarking or disembarking."

The Montreal Convention of 1999 sets up a two-tiered system of liability. The first tier requires the air carrier to pay up to 100,000 Special Drawing Rights (SDRs) regardless of whether or not the air carrier was negligent or otherwise at fault in any way. All the injured passenger or survivors of a deceased passenger need prove is that the passenger was in fact injured or killed, and that such injury or death was caused by an "accident." This is a form of absolute or strict liability, except that the air carrier can raise the defense that the passenger was also at fault ("contributory" or "comparative" fault) for his injuries or death. The second tier (i.e., claims above 100,000 SDRs) allows for unlimited recovery, up to the amount the victim can prove he suffered as a result of the injury or death. However, the air carrier is not liable if it can prove that the injury or death was not due to the negligence or other wrongful act or omission of the air carrier or its employees, or that the injury or death was solely due to the negligence or other wrongful acts or omissions of a third party.

The Montreal Convention went into force on November 4, 2003, the 60th day following the date of deposit of the instrument of ratification, acceptance, approval, or accession by the 30th country, the United States on September 5, 2003. As of August 2009, there were 92 signatories to the Montreal Convention, including most European countries, the European Union, Japan, Canada, Australia, China, Korea, Mexico, and the United States. The Montreal Convention has been ratified by those countries that cumulatively make up the largest share of international air transport. Under the Montreal Convention, the air carrier may agree to higher limits of liability, or even no limits on liability; however, it may not undercut the limits provided by the Montreal Convention. Additionally, the air carrier may waive defenses under the Montreal Convention.

Two conditions must exist in order to hold an airline liable for injuries or deaths arising in an international flight. First, there must be an "accident," which the United States Supreme Court has defined as a "happening or event"—including negative conduct, such as an omission or failure to do something, such as the failure of airline personnel to respond to a medical request of a passenger, resulting in the passenger's injury or death—that is external to the passenger, unexpected from the passenger's point of view, and not associated with the normal operation of the airplane. Second, there must be an actual physical or bodily injury. Mental anguish or emotional distress cannot be the sole basis for a claim. The Montreal Convention also does not allow the recovery of "punitive, exemplary or any non-compensatory damages." As mentioned above, the Montreal Convention also gives the air carrier the right to raise the passenger's own wrongful conduct ("contributory" or "comparative" negligence) as a defense to reduce or eliminate its liability.

Victims of air crash disasters are usually entitled to receive the full economic ("pecuniary") damages suffered. Pecuniary damages are those items of damage upon which a value can be reasonably placed, such as hospital and medical expenses, lost past and future wages, lost earning power, etc. Non-economic damages ("non-pecuniary") include such things as pain and suffering in the case of an injured passenger, and the loss of care, comfort, and society in the case of a passenger who is killed. Punitive and similar type damages are not recoverable. The right to all claim types is extinguished if not brought within two years from the arrival or date of scheduled arrival. The time limit is an absolute "condition precedent" to bringing a lawsuit and is not subject to extension.

The Montreal Convention of 1999 applies only if the trip involves a point of origin and point of ultimate destination in countries that are parties to the Convention. For instance, suppose the country Xanadu is not yet a party to the Montreal Convention. An Air Xanadu flight ticketed from Xanadu to San Francisco International Airport with a return to Xanadu is not governed by the Montreal Convention, since Xanadu is not a party to the Convention. However, a passenger on an Air Xanadu flight ticketed from San Francisco to Xanadu with a return to San Francisco would be governed by the Montreal Convention of 1999, because the point of origin and point of ultimate destination is in the United States (a contracting State), with an agreed stopping place in Xanadu (a non-contracting State).

The Montreal Convention and Warsaw System apply only to international air carriers and do not control damage claims by victims against other defendants. For instance, if the crash is due to a faulty design or manufacturer of a component in the airplane, the victim or his survivors can sue the manufacturer of the airplane and/or the manufacturer and supplier of the component part for all damages they can prove, without limitation. Airports, private security companies, and other service providers can be sued without having to worry about the Montreal Convention or Warsaw System's limitations on damage. Indeed, even the United States can be sued without limitation for, e.g., the negligence of its air traffic controllers.

FATAL CRASHES AT SEA

If a passenger dies in an aircraft crash on or above the "high seas," the Death on the High Seas Act (DOHSA) applies in United States courts. Under admiralty law, the survivor's damage was previously restricted to pecuniary loss only, that is, the financial loss the family suffers as the result of the death, reduced by the amount of expenses that would be incurred by the decedent. However, under the 2000 Death on the High Seas Amendment, the victim's family can now recover for the non-pecuniary loss of care, comfort, and companionship resulting from the death of their loved one in addition to such pecuniary damages as lost past and future wages. But recovery is still not permitted either by the families or the passenger's estate for the pre-impact pain and suffering suffered by the passenger in the airline disaster. The "high seas" are defined as the seas and oceans more than 12 miles from the shore of the United States and its islands. In most other countries, the high seas are defined as those seas more than three nautical miles off the country's shore.

If the aircraft crashes within 12 nautical miles of the shores of the United States and results in death, then the cases will be determined using the laws in effect in the various states and under federal law. Crashes on or above the high seas outside 12 nautical miles from the shores of the United States will fall within the Death on the High Seas Act.

26 CRUISE SHIP LIABILITY

Approximately 7 million people worldwide go on cruises every year. Some go on long-weekend three-day cruises, others take six-month cruises, while many take cruises of two to four weeks. While the vast majority of passengers will have a delightful, memorable, and uneventful cruise, for some the dream cruise they had been planning for months, if not years, turns into tragedy when they are seriously injured or killed due to the carelessness ("negligence") of the cruise line and its employees.

Any one of the following factors can cause injury or death, turning a fun cruise into a nightmare:

- "Slip and fall" or "trip and fall" incidents
- Hazardous decks, stairways, and walkways
- Inadequate ship maintenance
- Water slide, wave pool, and swimming pool accidents
- Contaminated food and food poisoning, resulting in serious injuries
- Passengers who fall overboard
- Unsafe doors that close too quickly or too forcefully
- Drownings
- Head and traumatic brain injuries

- Spinal cord injuries
- Infectious diseases and viruses
- Sexual or other physical assaults by crew members
- Explosions and fires
- Unseaworthy conditions
- Injuries incurred during on-shore activities and excursions arranged or sanctioned by the cruise ship company

THE INJURED PASSENGER'S RIGHTS

The legal rights of a passenger who has suffered an injury on a cruise ship, or of the heirs of a passenger who has been killed, depend largely on two things: maritime law and the provisions of the passenger's contract/ticket for carriage. Deaths occurring more than three miles off the United States' shore come under the jurisdiction of the Death on the High Seas Act (DOHSA), discussed separately. Under maritime law, a ship owner owes passengers a duty to take ordinary reasonable care under the circumstances.

YOUR TICKET AND CONTRACT
WITH THE CRUISE LINE

A passenger's contract/ticket is carefully drafted by the cruise line not only to tell you of your rights, but just as importantly— if not more so—to govern such things as what you can sue the cruise line for, the location where you must bring suit, how soon after the incident you must give written notice of your claim to the cruise line (usually six months), and the length of time you have to sue the cruise line (usually one year). What law applies to your ability to bring suit also depends on where the ship was at the time of the injury. For instance, the type and amount of damages you may be entitled to may vary greatly if the injury or death occurred while the ship was docked at Long Beach, was in Mexican territorial waters, or was on the high seas (more than three miles off most countries' shores).

A passenger's cruise ticket for an ocean voyage constitutes a maritime contract. Most ticket/contracts require that any lawsuits against the cruise ship must be filed only in certain places, usually cities or counties where the cruise line has its offices. The top places designated by the contract/ticket for filing a suit for personal injuries or death arising out of a domestic cruise ship's negligent conduct are Miami, Los Angeles, New York, and Seattle. For purely international cruises, such as a Mediterranean cruise aboard a Greek cruise ship, if you should be injured or a loved one killed on the cruise, you are probably going to have to prosecute the claim in Greece, even though the ticket was purchased in the United States. But if the passenger set off aboard a cruise line out of the Port of Miami and went on a Caribbean cruise and returned to the Port of Miami, chances are that the contract/ticket provides that lawsuits against the cruise line for injury or death must be brought in Florida.

In determining where you can and must file your lawsuit against the cruise line, the contract/ticket contains language of where you must sue the cruise line if you have been injured or a loved one killed on a cruise. The standard applied is that the ticket must reasonably communicate the existence of important terms and the passenger must have the opportunity to become meaningfully informed of those terms. The court will also look to the location of any restrictive provisions and simplicity of the language used to limit a passenger's rights.

The question boils down to whether, taken together, the various notices and provisions of the cruise contract/ticket are legally sufficient to give effect to the various liability and claim procedures it contains. For example, a passenger who claims that requiring the case to be filed thousands of miles away is unreasonable has a heavy burden of demonstrating why enforcement of the site specified by the contract/ticket is unreasonable. Whether the terms and conditions of the passage contract were reasonably communicated is a question of law for the court to determine.

TYPES OF DAMAGES RECOVERABLE

A cruise ship passenger who has been injured because of a cruise ship's employee's negligence is entitled to recover monetary damages for past, present, and future medical expenses, lost wages—both past and present—loss of earning power, and, if within three miles of the U.S. coastline, her pain and suffering and loss of enjoyment of life. Outside the limit of three nautical miles, the passenger must allege a physical injury to recover damages for purely emotional distress, mental anguish, and psychological injuries. In one case involving a cruise ship, approximately 210 passengers brought suit against the cruise line and its captain for extreme emotional distress. The gist of the cases was that their emotional injuries occurred because the captain sailed into bad weather that the ship's officer was aware of but did not avoid. The cruise line proved that some 140 of the passengers did not have any objective physical injuries and were therefore not entitled to recover for their purely emotional distress.

WHAT TO DO IF YOU HAVE BEEN INJURED

If you are injured or a loved one killed on a cruise ship, you should report your injury or loved one's death to the cruise ship employees as soon as possible. If there is a medical doctor or other health care professional aboard the ship, you should contact him for immediate treatment in the case of an injury. It may be necessary for you to be taken off the ship by a helicopter, or the ship may have to change its destination and head to the nearest port of call so that you can get prompt medical treatment.

If you are able to, take pictures of the area where you were injured. If you're not able to do it yourself, then you should instruct your spouse or traveling companion to take pictures for you. Don't forget to take pictures of your injuries. If you didn't bring a camera and your mobile phone doesn't take pictures, a disposable camera can be purchased in the ship's gift shop for around $10. If you are unable to do so, your spouse or traveling companion should get the names and addresses of all witnesses to the accident, and if possible, a brief statement from them relating what they saw. The cruise ship employees have a duty to assist you in collecting this information when you are unable to do so yourself.

If you have been injured or a loved one killed while aboard a cruise ship, you should contact a personal injury lawyer with experience in maritime law and cruise ship injuries and deaths as soon as possible so your claim is not barred by the "statute of limitations." The statute of limitations tells you how long you have to file a lawsuit in federal court or you will lose the right to sue forever. Maritime law and the contract/ticket with the cruise ship determine the amount of time you have to sue the cruise line for injuries or death. Although the normal time a person has to file under maritime law is three years, by signing the contract/ticket with the cruise line, that time is generally shortened to one year. And before you can bring a suit in court, the contract/ticket usually requires that you must first file a claim with the cruise line within six months of the incident.

The contract/ticket may also require you to submit a "Bill of Particulars" with your claim to the cruise ship within six months of the injury or death. Typically, in the Bill of Particulars you must send notice of your injuries or loved one's death and tell them why you feel the cruise line is liable to you. If a satisfactory settlement cannot be reached with the cruise line, you must file a lawsuit within one year of the incident. The ticket inevitably will provide that you must present your claim to the cruise line within six months, and if you don't, you lose your right to sue the cruise line forever. Unless your claim is very small, you should not attempt to negotiate with the cruise line itself. If you do send notice to the cruise line of your claim, you should send it and your Bill of Particulars via certified mail and request a return receipt to prove that you sent notice of your claim in on time. The cruise line is usually identified at the top of your ticket. Do not make the mistake of sending notice to the travel agent or ticket agent. The lawsuit is against the cruise line, and timely (i.e., usually six months) written notice of the accident and injury must be sent to it.

If your injuries are serious, or a passenger died on the cruise, you should contact an attorney promptly after you return home. An attorney experienced in cruise ship liability will know how, what, and where to file the notice and Bill of Particulars. Don't forget to gather your contract/ticket and all other written information, pamphlets, brochures, receipts, documents, and pictures so you will have them ready when you meet with your lawyer. If you are injured and unable to go to the lawyer's office, the lawyer will usually come to your home or the hospital. If your injuries are serious or a death is involved but you think you can handle the case yourself, think again. One respected study of injured and deceased victims demonstrated that, even after paying the lawyer's fees, injured persons who had lawyers handle their case for them ended up with more money in their pockets than people who handled their cases by themselves.

In cases involving injuries or deaths from dangerous conditions existing aboard the ship, a cruise line is liable for injuries to its passengers only where it has actual or implied ("constructive") notice of a dangerous condition. Without knowledge of any unreasonable risk or danger, the cruise line has no duty to warn of or remove the dangerous condition. In maritime law, constructive notice of an onboard dangerous condition is shown when it has existed long enough to give rise to an inference that crew members must have noticed it.

INJURIES OR DEATHS RESULTING FROM AN EXCURSION OR SIDE TRIP

Suppose you are on a cruise that stops at an island and offers passengers various excursions, from souvenir shopping to paragliding or Jet Skiing. One passenger goes out on the Jet Ski and is injured by another person on a Jet Ski that deliberately ran into her. Can the injured passenger sue the cruise line? Generally not.

The contract/ticket usually states that the cruise line is not liable for injury caused by any act not shown to be caused by its negligence or the negligence of its employees. The contract/ticket usually provides that shore excursions and other tours may be owned and/or operated by independent contractors and the cruise line makes no representation and assumes no liability for the wrongful conduct of the provider/operator of the shore excursion. The contract/ticket may state that if the passenger takes part in organized activities, whether on the ship or as part of a shore excursion, she assumes the risk of injury and the cruise ship is not liable or responsible for it.

DEATH ON THE HIGH SEAS

When a passenger has died, for example, due the negligence of an employee of a cruise ship, and the incident occurs within three nautical miles of the United States, the death is said to have occurred within the state's territorial waters and the wrongful death laws of the state apply. However, if the incident occurs more than three nautical miles off the U.S. coast, then the action is governed by the Death on the High Seas Act (DOHSA). In most such cases, DOHSA preempts general maritime law and limits the types of damages the heirs can recover.

DOHSA was originally enacted in 1920 to make it easier for widows of seamen to recover damages for future earnings when their husbands were killed in international waters. The cruise industry has since used the law to limit damages when a passenger aboard a cruise ship is killed on the high seas. In 2006, the Death on the High Seas Act was revised and reenacted (United States Code Title 46, sections 30301 et seq.). Under the new provisions, the Death on the High Seas Act states:

When the death of an individual is caused by wrongful act, neglect, or default occurring on the high seas beyond three nautical miles from the shore of the United States, the personal representative of the decedent may bring a civil action in admiralty against the person or vessel responsible. The action shall be for the exclusive benefit of the decedent's spouse, parent, child, or dependent relative.

DAMAGES YOU CAN SUE FOR UNDER DOHSA

Damages under DOHSA are primarily determined based upon the actual or projected value of the financial benefit that would have been received from the decedent, so-called "pecuniary damages." A spouse can recover for the actual value of the financial contribution the deceased spouse would have made to the family had he lived, reduced by the amount determined to have provided for the care and maintenance of the decedent personally. DOHSA does not provide for a loss of society or consortium, but the surviving spouse and dependents can recover for the monetary value of the household services the decedent would have provided. This portion of recovery is based on the number of hours the beneficiaries would have expected to receive in services from the decedent and are calculated based upon an hourly rate for those services projected over the decedent's life expectancy.

Under the 2000 Death on the High Seas Amendment, the victim's family can recover for the non-pecuniary loss of care, comfort, and companionship resulting from the death of their loved one in addition to such pecuniary damages as lost past and future wages. But recovery is still not permitted either by the families or the passenger's estate for the pre-impact pain and suffering experienced by the passenger in the cruise line disaster.

Under the 2000 amendment, dependent children can recover for the value of parental care, nurturing, training, and guidance they would have received from the deceased parent, as well as the loss of an expected inheritance. Pecuniary damages for the death of a loved one include pre-death medical expenses, as well as funeral and burial costs. However, DOHSA does not authorize recovery for non-pecuniary losses, such as pre-death pain and suffering (in most cases), loss of comfort and society, grief, sorrow, and other "intangible," or non-pecuniary, damages. The only damages available to other eligible persons (parents and dependent relatives) are the lost monetary sums the deceased person would have contributed to them had he survived. Under DOHSA, a lost monetary sums claim related to an older, retired person who is not employed, or a child who is not working, would likely result in only minimal damages, since they were not making any or much money or making a significant financial contribution to the family.

SURVIVAL ACTIONS NOT ALLOWED

DOHSA does not allow for a "survival" action. A survival action covers the period from the time the person is injured until she dies. For example, if a person is severely injured and suffers intense pain for two weeks before succumbing to her injuries, the survivors are not allowed to bring a survival action to get compensated for the physical and emotional pain and suffering their loved one endured before dying. (They would, however, be able to recover the medical expenses incurred during this time as they are pecuniary damages.) The exception to the rule that damages for pre-death pain and suffering are not recoverable is that, if an injured person files a DOHSA lawsuit and dies before it is resolved, the personal representative of the deceased person can be substituted as the plaintiff and the lawsuit is not otherwise affected.

RESTRICTIONS REGARDING THE FILING OF A DOHSA LAWSUIT

Actions based on DOHSA must be filed within three years, although cruise lines may shorten that time to as little as one year in their contract/ticket. DOHSA lawsuits can only be brought by a deceased person's personal representative, for the exclusive benefit of the decedent's spouse, parent(s), child(ren), and dependent relative(s). Additionally, before a DOHSA lawsuit may be filed, the ticket/contract with the cruise line often requires that the cruise line be given notice within six months after the injury or death of the passenger, along with a "Bill of Particulars"—a statement of what injuries the passenger suffered and what the alleged cause(s) of such injury were or what the bases are for holding the cruise line liable for the death of the passenger.

Where the DOHSA case must be filed does not depend on where the person lives. Rather, it depends on where the negligent act that ultimately caused the death occurred. So if the person was injured on the high seas but taken to a hospital in California where he died of the injuries, the case is governed by DOHSA rather than California state law. In the case of cruise ships, usually the place(s) where the cruise line can be sued is specified on the contract/ticket.

Suppose a personal representative files a DOHSA lawsuit on behalf of a widow and her three children. The case is successful and a single monetary amount is awarded. How is the award divided among the four plaintiffs? It is up to the court (i.e., the judge) to apportion the recovery among those individuals in proportion to the loss each has sustained.

PART VII:
INJURIES AND DAMAGES

27 WHIPLASH AND SOFT-TISSUE INJURIES

Whiplash has been the butt of many jokes and parodies over the years. However, the fact is that it can be a serious injury requiring medical attention and extensive physical therapy. Whiplash occurs when the head is snapped suddenly and violently forward then backward, as would happen if you collided with a car that suddenly pulled out in front of you. Severe whiplash can result in injury to the intervertebral joints, discs, ligaments, and nerve cases. In especially severe cases of whiplash, surgery may be necessary to repair damage to the soft tissue. Between 15 and 40 percent of people who suffer whiplash will continue to have pain months after the injury was sustained. There is an 18 percent chance that a whiplash victim will still be experiencing some symptoms more than two years after the accident.

Whiplash injuries may not show up right away; a person may awaken several days or a week or two later with classic signs of whiplash, such as neck pain, shoulder stiffness, and headache. Usually, the sooner the symptoms of whiplash appear, the more serious the injuries tend to be. Depending on the severity of the whiplash, the doctor may order the patient to wear a cervical (neck) collar, take anti-inflammatory drugs such as aspirin, ibuprofen (e.g., Advil or Motrin), or naproxen (Aleve).

For people who are suffering greater than normal pain, the doctor may prescribe strong prescription pain relievers, such as Vicodin and Norco, as well as muscle relaxants. The doctor may also prescribe physical therapy for the victim for a period of several months or more, depending upon how the victim is recovering. While the majority of whiplash victims recover in six to twelve weeks, for some people, regardless of the brace, medications, and physical therapy, whiplash results in long-term symptoms which can be extremely painful and disabling.

In addition to "simple" whiplash, there is the more serious Whiplash-Associated Disorder (WAD). In the more severe and chronic cases of WAD, the person may experience depression, anger, frustration, anxiety, stress, drug dependency, alcoholism, substance abuse, Posttraumatic Stress Disorder (PTSD), insomnia, and social isolation. In some cases, the snapping motion of the neck is so strong that it may cause the dislocation or even a fracture to a cervical vertebra, causing paralysis. (See Chapter 29 for a discussion of Spinal Cord Injuries.)

28 BROKEN BONES

If you were injured in an automobile collision or other type of accident caused by another person that resulted in broken bones, you have the right to recover monetary compensation for all of your injuries and associated costs. Common causes of bone fractures include motor vehicle accidents, falls from a height, a direct blow to the bone, child abuse, and repetitive forces, such as those produced by running, causing stress fractures of the foot, ankle, tibia, or hip.

One source says that the most commonly fractured bone is the collar bone ("clavicle"), usually as the result of an automobile accident. Another source lists breaks of the wrist, hip, and ankle as the most common fractures. A break or a crack in a bone is known as a fracture and can affect any bone in the body. A simple (or "closed") fracture is a clean break to the bone that does not damage any surrounding tissue or break through the skin. The only way of certainty in diagnosing a closed fracture is with an X-ray, CT scan, or MRI.

A compound (or "open") fracture occurs when the surrounding soft tissue and skin is damaged, such as where the broken bone penetrates through the skin. The attending emergency room physician will order X-rays or other imaging studies performed so she can find out exactly the extent of injury. This kind of fracture is more serious in large part because there is a high risk of infection since it is an open wound.

Additionally, a "simple" fracture is one that occurs along one line, splitting the bone into two pieces, while "multi-fragmentary" fractures, known as "comminuted fractures," involve the bone splitting into multiple pieces. A simple closed fracture is much easier to treat and has a much better prognosis for full recovery than an open comminuted fracture. Another type of bone fracture is a "compression fracture," which usually occurs in the vertebrae (the bones that make up the spinal column). There are approximately 14 different types of fractures.

Fractures are most frequently a result of an accident such as a bad fall or motor vehicle collision. The time it takes for a bone to heal depends on the type of fracture, where it is, and if it is an open or closed fracture. Healing of a broken bone is a gradual process, and it can take anywhere from a few weeks to several months. The healing process may, in fact, take even longer in some cases, such as in the presence of chronic diseases like osteoporosis and diabetes. As a person gets older, their bones become weaker making the individual more prone to fractures if they fall. Young children get different types of fractures because their bones are more elastic. They also have growth plates at the ends of the bones that can be damaged.

In order for a fracture to heal as well as possible, a good placement ("reduction") of the bones must be attained. When doctors talk about "reduction" of a fracture, or "reducing" the broken bone, they are talking about improving the alignment of the broken ends of the bone. In most cases reducing a fracture may involve a little pulling and tugging of the bones to attain optimal alignment. Once the bones are properly aligned, a plaster or fiberglass cast will be applied to hold the bones in the proper position while they heal.

A plaster cast molds to the skin better and is preferred if the broken bone needs to be held in a specific place. If the fracture is not unstable, or if some healing has already taken place, a fiberglass cast may be used. In many cases, physical therapy is required after the fracture has healed and the cast is taken off to strengthen the muscles and restore mobility in the affected area. Fractures near or through joints may result in the joint becoming permanently stiff or being unable to bend properly. In such a case, the lawyer will argue that the patient/client is entitled to recover a higher monetary award to compensate the injured person for the added pain and suffering, lack of enjoyment of life, and work prohibitions that the victim will experience.

If the bones cannot be properly aligned or are not sufficiently stable, and reduction cannot be satisfactorily achieved, then surgery is often necessary. In one type of surgery, "internal fixation," an orthopedic surgeon aligns the fractured bones with pins, plates, screws, or rods. A second type is "external fixation." Here, the pins or screws are placed into the broken bone above and below the fracture site. The orthopedic surgeon then repositions the bone fragments, and the pins or screws are connected to a metal bar or bars outside the skin. The external fixation devices hold the bones in the proper position so they can heal. After an appropriate amount of time, the external fixation devices are removed.

Occasionally the orthopedic surgeon uses "bone grafting" to treat a fracture. A bone graft is surgery to place new bone into spaces around a broken bone or bone defects. The new bone can be taken from the patient's own healthy bone (an "autograft"), from frozen, donated bone ("allograft"), or an artificial, synthetic, or natural substitute for bone. Bone grafting is used to repair bone fractures that are extremely complex, pose a significant health risk to the patient, or fail to heal properly. The new bone is held in place with pins, plates, or screws. Stitches are used to close the wound, and a splint or cast is usually used to prevent injury or movement while the bone is healing.

Bone grafts are used to fuse joints to prevent movement, repair broken bones (fractures) that have bone loss, and to repair bone that has not healed. Surgeons use bone grafts to repair and rebuild diseased bones in the hips, knees, spines, and sometimes other bones and joints. Most bone grafts help the bone defect to heal with little risk of graft rejection, and recovery time generally varies from two weeks to two months, depending on the injury or defect being treated. Vigorous exercise is usually prohibited for up to six months.

If you have suffered a broken bone due to another person's carelessness ("negligence"), you are entitled to recover your medical expenses, lost wages, pain and suffering, and loss of enjoyment of life you endured from the party that negligently injured you, as well as the lost wages for the time you are off work for surgery, recovery, and physical therapy. Recoverable medical expenses include visits to the emergency room, your primary care provider, an orthopedic specialist, and the costs of having a cast made for you. If the break results in a deformity or limp that you will have to live with for the rest of your life, you are entitled to receive damages for that as well.

29 SPINAL CORD INJURIES: QUADRIPLEGIA AND PARAPLEGIA

If you suffer an injury that severs or compresses the spinal cord in your neck or back, there is a good chance that you will be paralyzed from the point of injury downward for the rest of your life. This is called a "spinal cord injury," or SCI for short. A little neurology and anatomy will be of immense help here.

The central nervous system (CNS) is made up of two parts: the brain and the spinal cord. The spinal cord runs from the base of the brain down the back to the tailbone. The spinal cord is protected by the spinal column, which consists of bones with a hole in the middle of them. These bones are called the vertebrae. At the top of the spinal cord are seven vertebrae known as the cervical vertebrae (C-1 to C-7, in descending order). Running down the back are the 12 "thoracic" vertebrae (T-1 to T-12), which are in turn followed by the five "lumbar" vertebrae (L-1 to L-5). The "sacrum" (S-1 to S-5) and the "coccyx" (tailbone) make up the remainder of the spinal column. Injuries to the cervical spine resulting in paralysis of the body below a certain point are known as quadriplegia (also called tetraplegia), while injuries to the spinal column at or below the thoracic level are classified as paraplegia.

The cervical spinal nerves control signals to the back of the head, the neck and shoulders, the arms and hands, and the diaphragm. The thoracic spinal nerves control signals to the chest muscles, some muscles of the back, and parts of the abdomen. The lumbar spinal nerves control signals to the lower part of the abdomen and the back, the buttocks, some parts of the external sex organs, and parts of the leg. Sacral spinal nerves control signals to the thighs and lower parts of the legs, the feet, most of the external sex organs, and the area around the anus. As you can see, the higher the SCI to the spine, the more disabling—and potentially fatal—the injury. For instance, a spinal cord injury at the neck level may cause paralysis in both arms and legs and make it impossible for the victim to breathe without a respirator, while a lower injury may affect only the legs and lower parts of the body.

SCIs involving the cervical vertebrae usually cause loss of function in the arms and legs, known as quadriplegia (or tetraplegia). If the SCI is at or above the C-3 level (C-1 to C-3), then the ability to breathe on one's own is affected, and it will probably be necessary to have a mechanical ventilator for the person to breathe, as was the case for actor Christopher Reeve after his tragic accident until his death. Many people with SCI at or above C-3 die before receiving medical treatment because of their inability to breathe. C-4 is a critical level, as it is the level where nerves to the diaphragm—the main muscle that allows us to breathe—exit the spinal cord and go to the breathing center.

Besides allowing for regulation of the breathing process, injuries at C-4 may also allow the person some use of his biceps and shoulders, but this will be fairly weak. Injuries at the C-5 level often result in shoulder and biceps control, but no control of the wrist or hands. If the SCI is at the C-6 level, the victim usually has wrist control, but no hand function. Victims with SCI at the C-7 level can usually straighten their arms, but may still have dexterity problems with the hands and fingers. Injury at or below the C-7 level is generally considered to be the level for functional independence.

If the SCI is at the T-1 to T-8 levels, the victim usually has control of his hands, but poor trunk control resulting from a lack of abdominal muscle control. Lower thoracic vertebra injuries (L-9 to L-12) allow good trunk control and good abdominal muscle control, and the victim's sitting balance is very good. SCI to the lumbar and sacral regions result in decreasing control of the legs and hips, urinary system, and anus.

It is often impossible for the doctor to make a precise prognosis right away, and emergency doctors are advised not to make prognoses on the question of paralysis. There is no cure for an SCI, but the sooner the intervention, the better the chances of minimizing the damage. For example, a corticosteroid drug (methylprednisolone) administered within eight hours of the time of injury may reduce swelling, which is a common cause of secondary damage. An experimental drug currently being studied appears to reduce loss of function.

On about the third day of hospitalization following the injury-producing incident, the doctors give the victim a complete neurological examination to determine the severity of the injury and predict the likely extent of recovery. X-rays, CT scans, MRIs, and more advanced imaging techniques are also used to visualize the entire length of the spine.

Recovery, if it occurs, typically starts between a week and six months after the injury is sustained, especially as the swelling goes down. The majority of recovery occurs within the first six months after injury. Impairment remaining after 12 to 24 months is usually permanent, although with incomplete SCIs, the person may recover some functioning as late as 18 months after the injury. However, some people experience small improvements for up to two years or longer. For instance, Christopher Reeve regained the ability to move his fingers and wrists and feel sensations more than five years after he sustained a SCI to his cervical spine in a horse-riding accident. But the fact remains that only a very small fraction of persons who sustain an SCI will recover significant functioning.

Besides a loss of motor functioning and feeling below the level of injury, depending upon the level of the SCI, persons with SCI may experience other difficulties, such as:

- Pain or an intense stinging sensation caused by damage to the nerve fibers in the spinal cord
- Loss of sensation, including the ability to feel heat, cold, and touch
- Difficulty breathing, coughing, or clearing secretions from the lungs
- Loss of bladder or bowel control
- Pressure sores from sitting or lying in the same position for a long period of time (also called bedsores or "decubitus ulcers")
- Inability or reduced ability to regulate heart rate, arrhythmias (irregular heart beats), blood pressure, sweating, and, hence, body temperature
- Exaggerated reflex activities or spasms (spasticity)
- Atrophy of the muscles
- Blood clots, especially in the lower limbs (e.g., Deep Vein Thrombosis, commonly known as DVT) and in the lungs (pulmonary embolism
- Osteoporosis (loss of calcium) and bone degeneration
- Mental depression, often resulting in suicide or attempted suicide

The damage to the nerve may be complete or incomplete. With complete damage, there is a total loss of sensory and motor function below the level of the SCI; there is no movement and no feeling below the level of injury, and both sides of the body are equally affected. With incomplete damage, there is some functioning and/or sensation below the site of the SCI. For instance, a person with incomplete damage may be able to move one leg more than the other, may be able to feel parts of the body that cannot be moved, or may have more functioning on one side of the body than the other. The extent of an incomplete spinal cord injury is generally determined after spinal shock has subsided, approximately six to eight weeks after the injury is sustained. With advances in acute treatment of SCI, incomplete injuries are becoming more common than complete SCI injuries.

Accidents involving automobiles, motorcycles, and other motor vehicles, especially with Sport Utility Vehicles (SUVs) and 15-passenger vans rolling over, are the most common causes of SCIs. Spinal cord injuries due to violent acts—such as being shot or stabbed—are the second-most common type of SCI, and they are the leading type of SCI in some urban settings in the United States. SCIs due to falls are the third-most common type, occurring most frequently in persons aged 65 years or older. Recreational sports injuries (discussed in Chapter 15) are the fourth-most common cause of SCIs, with diving in shallow water being the sport that causes the most SCIs of all recreational sports, followed by impact in high-risk sports such as football, rugby, wrestling, gymnastics, surfing, ice hockey, and downhill skiing.

There is the risk of an earlier death for a person who suffers a SCI. The most common cause of death of SCI victims is diseases of the respiratory system, especially pneumonia. The second leading cause of death is non-ischemic heart disease; this almost always involves unexplained heart attacks, often occurring among young persons who have no previous history of underlying heart disease. Suicide is the cause of death in a substantial number of persons who sustain a SCI. Other leading causes of death involving an SCI are pulmonary emboli and septicemia (infection of the blood stream). Death rates are significantly higher during the first year after injury than during subsequent years, particularly for severely injured persons.

The financial and emotional costs associated with paraplegia and quadriplegia are enormous. The average length of the initial hospitalization following injury in acute care units is 15 days. The average stay in a rehabilitation unit is 44 days. The victim of a serious SCI will often have to go through extensive and exhaustive rehabilitation and physical therapy. Persons suffering from a serious SCI are generally treated at a regional SCI spine center. The initial hospitalization costs following an SCI are in the range of several hundred thousand dollars for paraplegics and over half a million dollars for quadriplegics. The average lifetime medical costs for victims becoming paraplegics at the age of 25 can easily top $1 million. The average lifetime costs for victims who become quadriplegics at age 25 easily reaches into the area of several million dollars.

30 TRAUMATIC BRAIN INJURIES

A person who suffers a severe blow or jolt to the head or a penetrating head injury may frequently develop a condition that disrupts the function of the brain. This is known as a traumatic brain injury (TBI). Auto accidents are a leading cause of TBIs, as are falls, such as a slip and fall accident in a grocery store or a trip and fall due to a defective walkway. TBI is a leading cause of death and disability in the United States. Each year, 1.4 million people sustain a traumatic brain injury. Fifty thousand of those die from the TBI, 235,000 people are hospitalized, and 1.1 million people are treated and released from an emergency room. The injury may be relatively minor, such as a minor concussion or brief period of unconsciousness, or it may be severe, such as a lengthy period of unconsciousness (a coma) or amnesia after the injury. Each year, 80,000 to 90,000 people will sustain a long-term disability as the result of a TBI. The Centers for Disease Control and Prevention estimate that at least 5.3 million Americans currently have a long-term or lifelong need for help to perform activities of daily living (ADLs) as a result of TBIs.

The leading causes of traumatic brain injury are falls and motor vehicle accidents, being struck by or against an object, and assaults by another person involving traumatic injury to the head. But TBIs need not be caused by a blow to the head. A violent jolt of the head such as one might experience in a rear-end collision ("whiplash") may result in serious brain injury. In a violent collision, the head snaps forward and the brain hits the front of the skull, then the head snaps backward and the brain hits the back of the skull. These impacts can cause a serious TBI. "Shaken-baby syndrome" is an example of a serious brain injury being inflicted without a direct blow to the head.

Even in this age of advanced medicine and neurobiology, there is no cure for a TBI. Improvement from a brain injury depends on the brain's "plasticity," that is, the brain's ability to "rewire" itself and have other areas of the brain take over the functions of the damaged areas.

Brains do not heal like broken limbs, and each person's brain is different. Although they may superficially appear alike, no two brain injuries are the same and the consequence of two similar traumatic brain injuries may be vastly different.

Health care professionals who deal with TBIs do not talk in terms of "recovery," but rather "improvement." The word "recovery" implies that that the effects of a TBI will disappear, whereas the reality is that improvement is usually all that can be expected. With a TBI, some of the effects may disappear after a couple of years or more, but more frequently these long-term changes linger on, changing only slowly—if at all—over the person's lifetime.

CATEGORIES OF TBI

TBIs are classified into three categories: mild, moderate, and severe.

1. Mild Traumatic Brain Injury A person with a mild TBI is one who has suffered trauma to the brain and: (a) had any period of loss of consciousness and/or confusion, (b) was disoriented or confused for less than 30 minutes, and/or (c) suffered from Posttraumatic Amnesia (PTA) (loss of memory for events immediately before or after the accident). Mild TBI is the most common type of TBI, and it is often missed at the time of the initial injury. Fifteen percent of people with mild TBIs have symptoms that last one year or more.

2. Moderate Traumatic Brain Injury Moderate TBI exists when a person has suffered trauma to the brain and: (a) lost consciousness for at least 20 minutes to six hours and/or (b) suffered from Posttraumatic Amnesia for more than 30 minutes but less than 24 hours. It also applies where the person has suffered a skull fracture. Moderate TBI may result in long-term physical or cognitive deficits, depending on the type and location of the brain injury. Rehabilitation will help to overcome some deficits and provide skills to cope with any remaining deficits.

3. Severe Traumatic Brain Injury A severe brain injury is a life-threatening condition in which: (a) the person loses consciousness for more than six hours or (b) has Post Traumatic Amnesia lasting longer than 24 hours. If the person lives, she will typically be faced with long-term physical and cognitive impairments, ranging from a persistent vegetative state to less severe impairments that may allow the person, with extensive rehabilitation, to continue to function independently.

DAMAGES DUE TO TBI

Symptoms common to mild TBIs include fatigue, headaches, visual disturbances, memory loss, poor attention and/or concentration, sleep disturbances, dizziness and/or loss of balance, irritability, feelings of depression, and, rarely, seizures. Other symptoms associated with mild TBIs include nausea, loss of smell, sensitivity to sound and lights, getting lost or confused, and slowness in thinking. Sometimes the cognitive symptoms are not readily identified at the time of the injury, but instead may show up as the person returns to work, school, or housekeeping. Friends and colleagues may notice changes in the person's behavior before the injured person realizes anything is wrong.

A person who has suffered a moderate or severe TBI may suffer from such cognitive deficits as difficulties with attention, concentration, distractibility, memory, speed of processing information, confusion, impulsiveness, language processing, and what are often referred to as "executive functions." Executive functions refer to the complex processing of large amounts of intricate information that we need to function creatively, competently, and independently as beings in a complex world. After a severe TBI, the person may be unable to function well in her social roles because of difficulty in planning ahead, keeping track of time, coordinating complex events, making decisions based on broad input, adapting to changes in life, and otherwise "being the executive" in her own life.

Some of the difficulties resulting from a moderate to severe TBI include speech and language problems, such as not understanding the spoken word, difficulty speaking and being understood, slurred speech, speaking very fast or very slowly, and issues with reading and writing. Sensory problems include difficulties with the interpretation of touch, being aware of changes in the temperature, and limb position. Partial or total loss of vision, weakness of eye muscles and double vision, blurred vision, difficulties judging distance, involuntary eye movements, and intolerance of light are other problems frequently found with moderate to severe TBIs.

Physical changes include paralysis, chronic pain, loss of bowel and bladder control, sleep disorders, loss of stamina, changes in appetite, difficulty regulating body temperature, and menstrual problems. Moderate to severe TBIs can cause a wide range of functional changes affecting thinking, language, learning, emotions, behavior, and sensation. TBIs can also cause seizures and increase the risk for such conditions as Alzheimer's disease, Parkinson's disease, and other brain disorders that become more likely as the person grows older.

A common complaint among persons who sustain a TBI is fatigue. Studies of people with TBIs found that between 37 and 98 percent of them said they had some type of fatigue. There are three types of fatigue: (1) physical fatigue: feeling tired and a need to rest and having muscle weakness, (2) psychological fatigue, in which the person can't get motivated to do anything, is often accompanied with depression (50-60 percent of people who suffer a TBI develop major depression, which affects only about 5 percent of the general population at any one time), anxiety (about twice the rate of the general population), Posttraumatic Stress Disorder (PTSD) and other psychological conditions, which may take months or years of psychotherapy to treat and may require psychoactive medication, and (3) mental or cognitive fatigue, in which the person has difficulty concentrating and finds it hard to stay focused, becomes irritable, or has headaches.

LONG TERM EFFECTS OF TBI

The long-term effects of a TBI depend on a number of factors, including: (1) the severity of the initial injury, (2) the rate and completeness of physiological healing, (3) the types of functions affected, (4) the resources available to aid in the recovery of function, and other factors. Most spontaneous improvement from a TBI occurs within the first month after a brain injury. Some additional gains may occur over the next three to six months. The long-term effects of a TBI are different for every person. Some may experience only subtle difficulties, others will have moderate dysfunction, while to still others the TBI may be life-threatening. With TBIs, the systems in the brain that control our social-emotional lives are often damaged. The consequences for the individual and his significant others may be very difficult, as these changes may imply to them that "the person who once was" is no longer there. Personality can be substantially or subtly modified following injury. The person who was once an optimist may now be depressed. The previously tactful and socially skilled negotiator may now be blurting comments that embarrass those around them. The person may also be characterized by a variety of other behaviors: dependent behaviors, emotional swings, lack of motivation, irritability, aggression, lethargy, lack of inhibition, and being unable to modify behavior to fit varying situations.

The severity of the injury and the resulting direct effects on the individual's body systems and cognitive abilities may not predict the amount of impact the TBI has on a person's life. For example, a severe injury to the frontal brain area may have less impact on an agricultural worker's job performance than a relatively mild frontal injury would have on a physicist's work. Hence, the extent of injury and damages in a specific person's life will depend on his pre-injury lifestyle, personality, goals, values, and resources, as well as his ability to adapt to changes and to learn techniques for minimizing the effects of brain injury.

WORKING WITH A LAWYER

If you or a loved one has suffered a traumatic brain injury due to another person's carelessness—such as an automobile accident caused by another person's inattentiveness or a slip and fall on a store's slippery floor—it is important that you promptly seek representation by a personal injury law firm experienced in this type of injury. Monetary damages you are entitled to receive when you have sustained a traumatic brain injury include all of your medical and rehabilitation costs, lost wages because you were unable to return to work, loss of enjoyment of life due to your impaired condition, pain and suffering, and psychological damage.

31 BURN INJURIES

Approximately 2.4 million burn injuries are reported each year. About 650,000 of the injuries are treated by health care professionals. Approximately 75,000 burn victims are hospitalized each year. Of those hospitalized, 20,000 have major burns involving at least 25 percent of their total body surface. Between 8,000 and 12,000 patients with burns die, and several hundred thousand sustain substantial or permanent disabilities resulting from these injuries. Burn injuries are the second leading source of accidental death in the United States, following only the number of deaths resulting from motor vehicle accidents.

TYPES OF BURNS

There are five major of types of burns: thermal burns, friction burns, electrical burns, chemical burns, and radiation burns.

1. Thermal Burns These are the most frequent type of burns and are caused by fire or excessive heat coming from such sources as steam, hot liquids, or contact with hot objects. In automobile collisions or motorcycle accidents, there is always the risk of a ruptured gas tank or loosened gas line igniting and catching fire, burning the people in the vicinity. Even when the person is removed from the source of the thermal burn, damage to his skin is still taking place and therefore the prompt administration of first aid is required. Depending upon their severity, thermal burns can cause anywhere from the minor discomfort of first-degree burns to life-threatening third-degree burns. In thermal burns, as well as other types of burns, the swelling and blistering of the burned skin is caused by the loss of fluid from damaged blood vessels. In severe cases, such fluid loss can cause shock. Immediate blood transfusion and/or intravenous fluids may be needed to maintain blood pressure. Due to the damage to the skin's protective barrier, burns often lead to infection, which, if not treated promptly and appropriately, can result in life-threatening consequences, even death.

A. Inhalation Burns Fire and heat have been associated with several types of inhalation injuries as well as burns to the flesh. (Inhalation injuries also occur with different types of burns, such as the inhalation of a caustic chemical.) When inhalation injuries are combined with external burns, the chance of death increases significantly.

The three types of inhalation injuries are:

1. Damage from Heat Inhalation True lung burns occur only if the person directly breathes in hot air or a flame source, or high pressure forces the heat into him. In most cases, thermal injury is confined to the upper airways. However, secondary airway injury can occur if a person inhales steam, as it has a greater thermal capacity than dry air.

2. Damage from Systemic Toxins Systemic toxins affect our ability to absorb oxygen. If someone is found unconscious or acting confused in the surroundings of an enclosed fire, the inhalation of systemic toxins could be a possible cause. More than a hundred known toxic substances have been identified in fire smoke. Toxin poisoning can cause permanent damage to internal organs, including the brain. Carbon monoxide poisoning can appear without symptoms up until the point where the victim falls into a coma.

3. Damage from Smoke Inhalation Injuries that were caused by inhaling smoke can easily be missed because of more visible injuries, such as burns as a result of the fire. Sometimes this leads to the victim not receiving the necessary medical treatment due to the rescue teams taking care of the more severely burned victims whose injuries are more apparent. People who appear unharmed can collapse due to a major smoke inhalation. 60 to 80 percent of fatalities resulting from burn injuries are due to smoke inhalation. Signs of smoke inhalation injury usually appear within 2 to 48 hours after the burn occurred. Symptoms of smoke inhalation include: (1) fainting, (2) evidence of respiratory distress or upper airway obstruction, (3) soot around the mouth or nose, (4) singeing of nasal hairs, eyebrows, and/or eyelashes, and/or (5) burns around the face or neck. Upper airway swelling ("edema") is the earliest consequence of inhalation injury, and it is usually seen during the first 6 to 24 hours after the injury. Early obstruction of the upper airway is managed by intubation. Initial treatment consists of removing the patient from the smoke and allowing him to breathe air or oxygen.

2. Friction Burns This type of burn commonly occurs when a person is dragged along a surface. For instance, in a motor vehicle-motorcycle accident in which the motorcyclist is dragged a certain distance, he will likely sustain friction burns caused by the asphalt or cement unless he was wearing protective clothing. Joggers, pedestrians, and bicyclists are at high risk for friction burns when they are injured by an automobile or other motor vehicle. When a person has been dragged in an accident, he usually sustains abrasion injuries as well as a friction burn.

3. Electrical Burns Contact between a person and an exposed live wire line or other electrical source is the cause of electrical burns. Contact with a high-voltage power source often results in limbs being severely burned as the electricity seeks a way out of the body. With some voltage sources, the person is unable to release his grasp on the power line or object, often resulting in electrocution. Besides the damage to the skin and limbs, electrical burns can severely affect the internal organs as well.

4. Chemical Burns Chemical burns are caused by acids and other caustic substances, many of which are found in household cleaning products.

5. Radiation Burns Radiation burns are caused by exposure to the sun, tanning booths, sunlamps, X-rays, radiation treatment for cancer, and nuclear medicine.

DEGREES OF BURNS

The severity of burns has traditionally been described in terms of degree. First-degree burns are the most shallow (superficial), and they affect only the top layer of the skin, the epidermis. First-degree burns are red, moist, swollen, and painful, and such burns may result in peeling and in severe cases, shock. Second-degree burns extend into the middle layer of the skin, the dermis, and often affect the sweat glands and hair follicles. Second-degree burns are red, swollen, and painful, and they develop blisters that may ooze a clear fluid. The skin may be white or charred, and the person may go into shock. If a deep second-degree burn is not properly treated, swelling and decreased blood flow in the tissue can result in the burn receiving a third-degree burn classification as the body's condition worsens.

Third-degree burns involve all three layers of the skin—the epidermis, the dermis, and the fat layer—and usually destroy the nerve endings as well. In third-degree burns, the skin becomes leathery and may be white, black, or bright red, with coagulated blood vessels visible just below the skin surface. There is usually little pain with third-degree burns, as the nerves have been destroyed, but the victim may complain of pain. This pain is usually due to second-degree burns. Healing from third-degree burns is very slow due to the skin tissue and structures having been destroyed. Burns of this severity usually result in extensive scarring. There are also fourth-degree burns, which involve damage to muscle, tendon, and ligament tissue.

The categorization of burns in terms of degrees is being phased out in favor of one reflecting the need for surgical intervention. The new language refers to burns as superficial, superficial partial-thickness, deep partial-thickness, and full-thickness.

Twenty-five years ago, people who suffered burns over 25 percent or more of their bodies were likely to die of their injuries. Today, advances in medicine make it possible to save many victims who have been burned over 90 percent of their bodies. Of course, these survivors will have long-term impairment, disability, scarring, and disfigurement, and they may never get back to leading a normal life.

When burn damage is due to another person's negligence, that person must compensate the victim for all of her injuries: financial, physical, and emotional. Over half of serious burn victims are now treated in the approximately 200 hospitals or clinics specializing in burn treatment. Many hospitals now have trauma teams that are specially educated in the treatment and management of burns.

TYPES OF SCARS

As burns heal, scars develop. There are three major types of burn-related scars: (1) keloid (2) hypertrophic, and (3) contracture. Keloid scars are an overgrowth of scar tissue that grows beyond the site of the burn. Generally red or pink at first, they become a dark tan over time. They occur when the body continues to produce collagen, a tough fibrous protein, after the wound has healed. Keloid scars are thick, nodular, ridged, and itchy during formation and growth. Extensive keloids may become binding and limit the person's mobility. Additionally, clothing rubbing or other types of friction may irritate this type of scar. Dark-skinned people are more likely to develop keloid scars than those with fair skin, and the possible occurrence of keloid scars reduces with age. Keloid scars may be reduced in size by freezing (cryotherapy), external pressure, cortisone injections, steroid injections, radiation therapy, or surgical removal.

Hypertrophic scars are red, thick, and raised, but unlike keloid scars these do not develop beyond the site of injury or incision. Additionally, hypertrophic scars will improve over time. This time can be reduced with the use of steroid application or injections.

The third type of scar, a contracture scar, is a permanent tightening of skin that may affect the underlying muscles and tendons; this can limit mobility, and there can be possible damage or degeneration of the nerves. Contractures develop when normal elastic connective tissues are replaced with inelastic, fibrous tissue. This makes the tissues resistant to stretching and prevents normal movement of the affected area. Physical therapy, pressure, and exercise can help in controlling contracture burn scars in many cases. If these treatments do not control the effects of contracture scars, surgery may be required. A skin graft or a flap procedure may be performed. The doctor may recommend a newer procedure, such as Z-Plasty or tissue expansion.

SURGICAL PROCEDURES TO IMPROVE SCARS

There are two major types of surgical procedures that can help to conceal scarring and replace lost tissue for severe burn victims: (1) dermabrasion and (2) skin grafts.

Dermabrasion is a surgical procedure to improve, smooth, or minimize the appearance of scars, restore function, and correct disfigurement resulting from a burn injury. Even with dermabrasion, scars are permanent but their appearance will improve over time. Dermabrasion may be performed in a dermatologic surgeon's office or in an outpatient surgical facility.

A skin graft is a surgical procedure in which a piece of skin from one area of the person's body is transplanted to another area of the body. Skin from another person or animal may be used as a temporary cover for large burn areas to decrease fluid loss. The skin is taken from a donor site, which has healthy skin, and it is then implanted at the damaged recipient site. Skin grafts and flaps are more serious than other scar revision surgeries, such as dermabrasion. They are usually performed in a hospital under general anesthesia. Depending on the size of the area and severity of the injury, the treated area may need six weeks to several months to heal. Within 36 hours of the surgery, new blood vessels will begin to grow from the recipient area into the transplanted skin. Most grafts are successful, but some may require additional surgery if they do not heal properly.

The success of a skin graft can usually be determined within 72 hours of the surgery. If a graft survives the first 72 hours without an infection or trauma, the body in most cases will not reject the graft.

Before surgery, the recipient and donor sites must be free of infection and have a stable blood supply. Following the procedure, moving and stretching the recipient site must be avoided. Dressings need to be sterile and antibiotics may be prescribed to avoid infection.

For many severely burned persons, skin grafts using their own healthy skin are not possible. These patients tend to have very little healthy skin or they may not be strong enough for the surgery. When other sources of skin must be used, options can be cadaver skin or animal skin. The body will usually reject both of these procedures within a few days and the surgery will need to be performed again. A synthetic product called Dermagraft-TC is made from living human cells and it is being used now instead of cadaver skin. The FDA has approved Dermagraft-TC and two artificial "interactive" burn dressings for use in treating third-degree burns. Unlike traditional bandages, some new dressings promote wound healing by interacting directly with body tissues.

Other substitute skin products may become available soon. Already, in addition to artificial skin, there is cultured skin. Doctors are able to take a postage-stamp-sized piece of skin from the patient and grow the skin under special tissue culture conditions. From this small piece of skin, technicians can grow enough skin to cover nearly the entire body in just three weeks.

COST OF TREATMENT/GETTING LEGAL HELP

Serious burns are one of the most expensive catastrophic injuries to treat, and they can lead to lasting physical disability and emotional damages. For instance, a burn of 30 percent of total body area can cost several hundred thousand dollars in initial hospitalization costs and physician fees. For more extensive burns, there are additional significant costs, such as the cost of multiple hospital admissions for reconstruction and rehabilitation. Scars may heal physically but they remain visible and last emotionally. Hence, it is of utmost importance if you have been severely burned due to another person's carelessness, that you retain an experienced personal injury lawyer who understands serious burn injuries. This type of lawyer can help you get full compensation for the physical and emotional trauma associated with the burns. You are entitled to recover all of your medical expenses—past and future—lost wages, pain and suffering, loss of enjoyment of life, and other damages.

32 AMPUTATIONS

Traumatic injury is the most common reason for an amputation among people younger than 50. The leading causes of those injuries include motor vehicle and motorcycle accidents, farm machines, power tools, and factory/industrial machines and equipment. Another source can be products that are dangerously designed, do not have sufficient safety measures built in, and/or lack a properly placed "off" switch. Traumatic amputation usually occurs at the scene of the accident, when the limb is completely or partially severed. Sometimes the injured person will make it to the hospital with the limb still attached but so badly crushed or mangled that amputation is necessary.

The amputation may be of one or more toes or fingers, a foot or a hand, a leg below or above the knee, or an arm below or above the elbow. A person may sustain amputations of more than one limb, such as both legs, both arms, or one of each. For instance, when a person comes into contact with an exposed, downed high-voltage power line, it is not at all unusual for the person to suffer the amputation of more than one limb as the electricity seeks paths to leave the body. Hemicorporectomy, or amputation at the waist downward, is the most radical—and rare—of all the types of amputations.

The majority of trauma-related amputations are of the arms (approximately 65 percent compared to 35 percent for leg amputations), and men are at a significantly higher risk than women for trauma-related amputations. However, the number of amputations in women is on the rise, as is the age of the victim who requires an amputation. If an accident or other trauma results in the complete amputation of a limb (i.e., the body part is totally severed), that part sometimes can be reattached, especially when proper care is taken of the severed part and the stump. However, often the victim will have a better outcome from having a well-fitting, functional prosthesis than a nonfunctional reattached limb.

The long-term outcome for persons who have lost a limb has improved greatly due to a better understanding of the management of traumatic amputation, early emergency and critical care management, new surgical techniques, early rehabilitation, and new prosthetic designs. But make no mistake about it: the loss of a limb is still a serious injury that requires major changes to your life. No amount of money and no prosthesis can ever replace a natural, fully functional limb.

Severe and persistent pain can be a fact of life for someone who has suffered a traumatic amputation. Up to 80 percent of all amputees still experience pain in their residual limb (the "stump") and in the part that is now missing, known as "phantom pain." Doctors are unsure exactly how this works, but to the injured victim the phantom pain in his missing limb feels as real and painful as if the missing limb were still attached. Rather than feeling pain in the missing limb, some amputees feel only phantom sensations, such as itching, burning, aching, pressure, touch, wetness or dryness, hot or cold, or movement in the missing limb.

Pain management is essential to the proper medical treatment of amputees. There are two types of pain in amputation cases: acute and persistent. Acute pain is usually severe in intensity but lasts a relatively short time. Persistent pain generally ranges from mild to severe and lasts for long periods of time, sometimes years. In the beginning of treatment, when pain is new and at its peak, it may be necessary to prescribe a drug from that group of pain medications known as "opioids." This category of drugs includes morphine, oxycodone, and codeine. Because of the risk of becoming addicted to an opioid drug, after the critical stage has ended and the pain is less intense, the doctor may switch the victim to a non-steroidal anti-inflammatory drug (NSAID), such as ibuprofen (e.g., Advil or Motrin), aspirin, acetaminophen (Tylenol), or naproxen (Aleve). If severe pain persists despite the use of medications and physical therapy, the victim may be referred to a pain management doctor or clinic.

In many cases, a prosthesis (artificial limb) will enhance an amputee's mobility and ability to perform the "activities of daily living" (ADLs), such as using the restroom by themselves, dressing themselves, making their own meals, showering, brushing their teeth, etc. A prosthesis must be fitted to the individual and should be comfortable, functional, and cosmetically appealing. Training by a skilled physical and/or occupational therapist is necessary before and after receiving a prosthesis. This training will help to maximize the functional use of the artificial limb, and it will also help to prevent the development of bad habits that may be difficult to break later.

While advances in medical treatments and surgical techniques continue, over the past decade, improved outcomes following amputation have largely been the result of advances in prosthetic technology. For instance, for lower-limb (i.e., leg) amputees, the number of prosthetic feet that provide "dynamic response" and the ability to maneuver on uneven surfaces continues to increase. Additionally, at least one microprocessor-controlled prosthetic foot-ankle unit is now available. For above-the-knee amputees, there are currently five different prosthetic knee units that use microprocessor-control. These units allow for more normal knee motion and stability through computerized parts that monitor motions and forces and make extremely rapid real-time adjustments while walking. This results in improved walking ability that requires less effort.

For upper-limb (i.e., arm) amputees, the original body-powered (i.e., cable controlled) prosthetic designs remain in common use, are the most durable, and continue to improve. Although using electrical signals from the muscles ("myoelectric componentry") to control prostheses for the upper limb has been in use for over 40 years, this technology continues to advance, with associated further enhancements in function. To improve the ability of high-level (close to or through the shoulder) upper-limb amputees to use a myoelectric prosthesis, in 2006 a surgical technique called "targeted reinnervation" was introduced, in which motor and sensory nerves are transferred to the part of the body that needs healing in order to improve motor control and sensory feedback during prosthetic use. The application of this technique is still in its early stages.

In most cases, the amputation victim is measured for a prosthesis several weeks after surgery, when the wound has healed and the tissue swelling is decreased. The medical team will be concerned with maintaining the proper shape of the residual limb, as well as increasing overall strength and function. The amputee will most likely need to make several visits for adjustments with the professional who made the prosthesis (the prosthetist), as well as extensive training with a physical therapist to learn how to use it. They can help the amputee ease pressure areas, adjust alignment, work out any problems, and regain the skills the amputee needs to adapt to life after limb loss.

Some people are not good candidates for prostheses, and these amputees will need to rely on mobility devices, such as a wheelchair or crutches. For instance, a person who has had both legs amputated (a "bilateral" amputee) may opt for a wheelchair, while a person who has had only one leg amputated (a "unilateral" amputee) may opt for a prosthesis. Of course, a unilateral lower-limb amputee who has had a prosthesis made for her may find it useful to use a cane or crutches for balance and support in the early stages of walking. Whether to use a prosthesis or a mobility device such as a wheelchair may be an individual decision based on such factors as the person's age, balance, strength, and sense of security, as well as the location and extent of the amputation.

Once the amputee has been fitted for a prosthetic limb, has mastered (or is well on her way to mastering) its use, and feels comfortable with its function, this is not the end of the road for the amputee. She will still need to make periodic follow-up visits to her doctor and prosthetist as a normal part of her life. Proper fit of the socket and good alignment will ensure that the prosthesis is still useful to the amputee and is not causing her discomfort, pressure sores, or other problems. Artificial limbs can break down over time and with continued use, and changes in the physical shape and condition of the amputee's residual limb (i.e., the stump) may require the amputee to go in and have adjustments made to an old prosthesis or get a new one made. Even small problems with the prosthesis should be brought to the immediate attention of the prosthetist. That way, the issue can get attention before that small problem suddenly results in the failure of the prosthesis and becomes a large problem, resulting in further injury to the amputee.

After the amputee has had her surgery and has been fitted for an artificial limb, she will need to keep a focus on the care of the wound site and maintenance of the residual limb. Any skin opening, whether it be for surgery or due to an improperly fitted prosthesis, runs the risk of becoming infected by germs entering the bloodstream through the opening. Infections can cause tenderness or pain, fever, redness, swelling, and/or discharge. These infections can lead to further complications that will require medical intervention, even surgery. If the infection is not treated in a timely manner, it is possible that the infection will grow and spread, causing death.

The amputee will always need to pay special attention to the hygiene of her residual limb, as it will be enclosed in the socket or liner of the prosthesis and thus will be more prone to skin breakdown and infections. If an amputee suspects that she is getting an infection, she should promptly see her medical doctor before it gets out of hand. If you are being fitted for a prosthetic limb, ask your prosthetist for information on caring for your residual limb to prevent infections and what to do if you suspect you have one.

In addition to the intense physical pain and emotional discomfort, the victim may suffer severe psychological trauma that will require intensive and prolonged mental health care intervention. Studies show that civilians suffering the loss of a limb in, say, a traffic accident have a greater risk of experiencing serious psychological problems than servicemen and women who have suffered a traumatic amputation as a result of, for example, the explosion of a roadside explosive device while serving her country in the Middle East.

From a psychological viewpoint, losing a limb is one of the most traumatic psychic events and losses you can suffer. Initially, the victim will feel tremendous grief over the loss of the limb. When the amputation is due to another person's careless act, the victim will at some point usually feel anger, even rage, toward that person. And as time goes by, the victim may fall into a deep clinical depression stemming from the loss of the limb. A victim suffering from mental and emotional problems arising from the loss of a limb should be treated by a psychologist and/or psychiatrist. The victim will need psychotherapy and, particularly in the case of depression, psychoactive medication to treat her mental condition. An amputee may become so despondent over the loss of her limb(s) that she attempts or completes suicide.

33 PSYCHOLOGICAL INJURIES

Monetary compensation for psychological injuries such as Posttraumatic Stress Disorder (PTSD), depression, anxiety, and phobias needing professional help are recoverable in most cases with proper psychiatric or psychological care and the use of psychoactive medications in many cases.

In one automobile accident case, a father and his 16-year-old daughter were seriously injured in a horrendous head-on collision. However, a 15-year-old cousin who was sitting in the back seat with her seatbelt on escaped with just a few cuts and bruises. The newspaper that covered the crash dubbed her lack of serious injuries a "miracle." Fast forward six months: the father and daughter are well on their way to full recoveries. However, things could hardly be worse for the "miracle girl" who avoided any physical injury with nary a scratch.

Soon after the accident, the girl began getting anxious when riding in a car. These feelings of general anxiety progressed to full-blown panic attacks that prevented the girl from riding in a car at all. Eventually, the girl's anxiety and panic became so strong that she was afraid to leave the house without a safe companion, and she was becoming frightened of leaving the house even with a safe person. The girl had developed a psychiatric condition known as panic disorder with agoraphobia that rendered her housebound. While she needed mental health care to overcome her fears, the girl was too scared to leave home to travel to the office of a psychiatrist or psychologist. She also developed severe depression.

The point of this case is to demonstrate that even when a person escapes serious physical injury, he may develop severe psychological damages that significantly impair his functioning in and enjoyment of life. And it doesn't have to be a serious accident to cause severe psychological injuries.

People who get in serious accidents can develop Posttraumatic Stress Disorder (PTSD), the same type of anxiety that combat soldiers often develop. The person may suffer nightmares about being in the accident, wake up in the middle of a summer's night in a cold sweat, duck for cover at loud noises such as a car backfiring, etc.

Many people who have been involved in an accident develop major depressive disorder (MDD), even if they were not physically harmed or suffered only superficial physical injuries. The outgoing, high-achieving high school student who was a passenger in a car that was involved in an accident but escaped with only a few cuts and bruises may turn sullen, lose interest in activities she used to enjoy, sleep too much or too little, experience fatigue or tiredness throughout the day, feel worthless or guilty, or have a diminished ability to think or concentrate. At its most serious, depression may result in having recurrent thoughts of death and suicidal ideations. In the worst case scenario, if the depressed individual does not get adequate mental health care in time, she may commit suicide, all stemming from an accident she was involved in but didn't suffer any serious physical injuries.

Psychological damage resulting from another person's careless conduct is real, debilitating, and sometimes deadly. If you find that a family member or loved one is acting differently since he has been involved in an accident of any type, encourage that person to see a psychiatrist or a psychologist for a mental health evaluation. A psychiatrist is a medical doctor (M.D.), while a psychologist is either a Ph.D. or Psy.D. Only a psychiatrist can prescribe medication, such as antidepressants or anti-anxiety drugs. Without a proper mental health checkup, your loved one may suffer excruciating psychic pain and lose all interest in others, things he used to enjoy, and even life itself. With proper psychotherapy and/or psychoactive medication, your loved one should be back to his old self again in several months.

34 PAIN AND SUFFERING

In many personal injury cases, compensation for the physical pain and emotional suffering you experienced and will continue to suffer because of another person's negligence often constitute a significant portion of the damages you are entitled to receive. Indeed, monetary compensation for physical and psychological pain and suffering constitutes the lion's share of many personal injury awards. Note, however, that in medical malpractice cases, awards for pain and suffering (and other "non-economic" damages) are limited to $250,000.

The amount of compensation the jury will award for pain and suffering depends upon the type and nature of the injury. For instance, a jury will award a person who has suffered serious burns over 30 percent of her body a significantly higher amount of compensation for pain and suffering than it will award a person who has suffered a typical whiplash injury. Pain and suffering is a catch-all phrase that includes such things as:

- Past and future physical pain
- Mental suffering
- Loss of enjoyment of life
- Disfigurement
- Physical impairment

- Inconvenience
- Grief (except in wrongful death cases)
- Anxiety
- Fright
- Humiliation
- Discomfort
- Fear
- Anxiety
- Embarrassment
- Anguish
- Other emotional distress the victim has suffered and will continue to suffer in the future

The Texas Court of Appeals once stated, "In a world so full of pain and suffering, it is strange that no one has perfected a gauge that will accurately measure its value."

At the end of a personal injury trial, when giving the jury its instructions, the judge will inform the jury not to speculate and that neither emotion nor prejudice has a place in their deliberations. The judge further instructs the jury that the only award permissible in a personal injury case is one lump sum for all time, in precise, cold, hard dollars and cents. Continuing his instructions to the jury, the judge will say further that "pain and suffering," "ridicule," "humiliation," "embarrassment," and the like all shall be evaluated, and only "in terms of dollars and cents." Then, as the jurors expectantly wait for further instructions of what is the evaluator or yardstick of the pain and suffering they are to award, the "kilowatt" of pain and suffering, they learn that the judge can give them no such yardstick because none exists. Every case must be determined on its own merits.

After telling the jury that they must return a verdict only in "dollars and cents" for pain and suffering, one judge said: "Under the head of this matter of pain with suffering and humiliation, I am unable to give you any definite rule by which you can assess damages. However, the law allows jurors to assess damages for pain and suffering and humiliation. Nobody can measure pain and suffering in damages. No one can value them particularly. If a man said to you, 'What would you take to suffer this or that,' usually they would tell you they would not take anything. There is no way of measuring pain and suffering definitely. But I say to you, ladies and gentlemen of the jury, it is a proper measure of damages. The only thing I can say to you about assessing damages in this kind of case for pain and suffering is that it is just a question of plain common sense. One judge has said it was just a matter of plain horse sense, and that particular statement was approved by the Supreme Court. Allow just such a sum as you think should be allowed in dollars and cents."

Loss of enjoyment of life can be a major element of pain and suffering for which monetary compensation is available in a personal injury case. For example, assume that you're an active man in his mid-twenties, playing basketball and tennis several times a week and running in the occasional marathon or taking part in triathlons. Because of another person's carelessness, you suffer an injury to your right leg that, due to its severity, prevents you from engaging in the activities you used to enjoy. You are entitled to receive fair compensation for this "loss of enjoyment of life."

In California, the victim's lawyer cannot argue to the jury how much money they would take to trade shoes with the injured person and ask what they would charge or expect as compensation for the pain and suffering endured by the injured plaintiff if it happened to them. This is known as the "Golden Rule" argument and is considered prejudicial to the defendant.

The jury is instructed merely that they are required to award an amount for pain and suffering that is reasonable in light of the evidence admitted at the trial, and that they must not let bias, sympathy, prejudice, or public opinion influence their decision.

In one case, the plaintiff's lawyer, during closing argument, asked the jury to assess damages from their own perspective, to act as "a personal partisan advocate for the injured party, rather than any unbiased and unprejudiced weigher of the evidence." The appellate court found this was an improper argument, because it was essentially a plea to apply the Golden Rule standard.

However, although the law prevents the victim's lawyer from asking the jury to put themselves in the victim's place when the injury results in an injury that will cause the victim pain and suffering for the future, even for rest of his life, California law permits the victim's lawyer to argue a per diem standard to determine the amount of her client's compensation. Under the per diem rule, an amount for hourly or daily pain is multiplied by the number of hours or days of the plaintiff's life expectancy. For instance, the victim's attorney can argue that the injured victim is entitled to, say, $100 a day for his pain and suffering, multiplied by the plaintiff's life expectancy. This means that a person suffering $100 per day of pain and suffering would be entitled to compensation of $36,500 per year, multiplied by the number of years of his life expectancy. Thus, if the plaintiff's life expectancy is 10 years, the plaintiff would be allowed $365,000 for pain and suffering. If his life expectancy were 20 years, he would be allowed $730,000 and so forth.

As the California Supreme Court has stated, there is no definite standard or method of calculation prescribed by law by which to fix reasonable compensation for pain and suffering. No method is available to the jury by which it can objectively evaluate such damages, and no witness may express his subjective opinion on the matter. In a very real sense, the jury is asked to evaluate in terms of money a detriment for which monetary compensation cannot be ascertained with any demonstrable accuracy. Translating pain and suffering into dollars can, at best, be only an arbitrary allowance, and not a process of measurement, and consequently the judge can give the jury no standard to go by; the judge can only tell the jury to allow such amount as in their discretion they may consider reasonable. The chief reliance for reaching reasonable results in attempting to value suffering in terms of money must be the restraint and common sense of the jury.

The jury must impartially determine pain and suffering damages based upon evidence specific to the victim, as opposed to statistical data concerning the public at large. The only person whose pain and suffering is relevant in calculating a general damage award is the victim. How others would feel if placed in the victim's position is irrelevant.

35 DAMAGE TO YOUR VEHICLE AND ITS CONTENTS

Suppose that you are in an accident which is entirely the other driver's fault and your two-year-old car is totaled. Is the other driver responsible for buying you a new car? No. When a car or other personal property is damaged or destroyed, the measure of damages is: How much will it cost to fix it? If it can't be fixed, how much is its replacement value? For instance, let's say you paid $25,000 for your car two years ago, but the fair market value of a two-year-old car of the same make and model was $17,500 at the time of the accident that destroyed your car. Under these circumstances, the most you can recover from the other driver is only $17,500. This is true even though you are likely to still owe more on your car loan than $17,500. Or if the cost of repairing your vehicle after such an accident exceeds its fair market value, the defendant would nevertheless only have to pay you the fair market value of the vehicle.

Likewise, if any contents you had in your car were damaged or destroyed during the accident, the party at fault must compensate you for their fair market value at the time of the accident. If the party at fault is uninsured, you will ordinarily have to recover the value of the contents by submitting a claim to your homeowner's insurance company.

PART VIII:
THE CASE AGAINST
TORT REFORM

This book is all about a person's right to be fairly and fully compensated for his or her injuries—or the death of a loved one—caused by the carelessness of another person. Historically, when a person injures another person, if the parties can't agree to settle the case between themselves out of court, the injured victim has the right to have his or her case heard in an open trial in a court of law and decided by a fair and impartial jury of 12 unbiased members of the community. The right to a trial by jury is such a fundamental right to the American judicial system that the 7th Amendment to the United States Constitution guarantees the right to a trial by jury where the amount in controversy is more than $20.

Unfortunately, the right of an injured person, or the family of a person who was killed due to another person's negligence, to seek full justice in a court of law before a fair and impartial jury is under vigorous attack by insurance companies, doctors and other health care professionals, and other special interest groups who claim that the jury system has gotten out of hand. These groups clamor for limitations on who can sue and the amount of money they can recover, all in the name of "tort reform." They have spent hundreds of millions of dollars trying to convince legislators and the public that "trial lawyers"—the lawyers who represent the injured victim or the family of a deceased person—are to blame for this "litigation crisis" and that without these limitations, chaos will surely follow.

The attempt to make it harder for a victim to sue a wrongdoer and limit the amount of money he or she can recover has been going on for a long time. In the early 1970s, doctors and the companies that insure them against medical malpractice lawsuits threatened that, because of the alleged (and highly suspicious) number of frivolous lawsuits and purported astronomical jury awards against them, doctors would either "go bare" (practice without being insured for errors), retire, or move to a more doctor-friendly state. In reality, the number of patients injured by a doctor's carelessness who receive inadequate or no compensation for their injuries is far greater than the number of frivolous lawsuits and exorbitant awards. Nevertheless, as a result of the lobbying efforts of insurance companies, the medical profession, and others, the California legislature enacted the Medical Insurance Compensation and Reform Act of 1975 (MICRA), which brought about a number of changes to medical malpractice lawsuits, making it harder for the innocent patient to sue a doctor who made a mistake.

The most drastic provision of MICRA limits "non-economic" damages—things like pain and suffering, loss of enjoyment of life, loss of comfort and society, loss of a limb, or disfigurement—to $250,000. When MICRA took effect in 1975, $250,000 was a fairly substantial amount of money, but even then it was insufficient to adequately compensate the most seriously injured person. There is no provision in MICRA to tie in the $250,000 amount with the inflation rate, so today the most an injured patient can recover for pain and suffering and other non-economic damages is still only $250,000. In 2010 dollars, $250,000 is worth only about $62,500 in 1975 dollars. To equal the purchasing power of $250,000 in 1975, you would need around $1,007,000 in 2010.

Suppose an orthopedic surgeon made a mistake while operating on a patient's upper spine (composed of seven bones called the cervical vertebrae). As a result of the doctor's incompetence, the patient is paralyzed from the neck down. Although the innocent patient can recover for all of his or her medical expenses, including future medical expenses related to the doctor's negligence, the patient can recover no more than $250,000 for pain and suffering, loss of enjoyment of life, inconvenience, loss of comfort and society, and other non-monetary, yet invaluable, aspects of living a normal life.

Another example of the injustice of placing a $250,000 limit on the amount of non-economic damages an innocent victim can recover: A surgeon mistakenly removes a healthy kidney instead of the diseased one, resulting in the patient being limited in the activities she can engage in and requiring she undergo several hours of dialysis three times a week for the rest of her life or have a kidney transplant. Although the careless doctor must pay all of the woman's medical bills related to the mistake, the woman is limited to recovering only $250,000 for her pain and suffering, inability to do certain things, inconvenience of having to undergo regular and frequent dialysis, inability to bear children, etc.

California automobile insurance companies have been trying to get a similar provision passed to prevent an innocent victim from recovering more than $250,000 in non-economic damages. Suppose that a person suffers severe burn injuries to his face when a gas tank ruptures and catches fire in a traffic collision that was the other driver's fault. Even with extensive plastic surgery, the innocent victim's face will always be severely disfigured and he will have to spend the rest of his life being treated as a pariah, with people looking away from him and even crossing the street to avoid passing by him. Young children will see his hideously disfigured face and run away screaming. If the automobile manufacturers and their insurers had their way, non-economic damages would be limited to $250,000, which in many cases will never sufficiently compensate the victim for his non-economic damages.

California companies that insure automobile drivers have managed to get several laws passed that limit an innocent victim's right to sue the guilty party for certain types of damages. For example, if a person was legally intoxicated while driving a motor vehicle and gets into an accident caused solely by the other driver's carelessness, and was in no way, shape, or form at fault for the accident himself, nevertheless he cannot recover any monetary damages for "non-economic" damages, including money to compensate him for pain, suffering, inconvenience, physical impairment, disfigurement, and other non-pecuniary damages, even though he had done nothing wrong to cause the accident.

Similar California laws prohibit the driver of a vehicle and its owner from obtaining any non-economic damages if she did not have the minimum amount of automobile insurance coverage at the time of the accident, even though she did not cause or contribute to the accident. However, if an uninsured driver was injured by the negligence of another driver who was operating his vehicle while under the influence of alcohol or other substance, the injured uninsured person may recover non-economic losses to compensate her for pain, suffering, inconvenience, physical impairment, disfigurement, and other nonpecuniary damages.

The reverse is not true, however. An intoxicated driver who is injured in an automobile accident caused by an uninsured driver is not permitted to recover non-economic damages for his pain and suffering, loss of enjoyment of life, and other such damages, even though he was clearly in the right and did not cause or contribute to the accident. Thus, if an intoxicated driver is stopped at a red light when he is rear-ended by another car traveling at a high rate of speed, resulting in serious and painful injuries, he is not allowed to recover any non-economic damages for his pain and suffering and other damages because he was intoxicated, even though his intoxication played no part in the accident. The legislature has decided that driving while intoxicated is a much greater evil than driving without insurance.

Tort "reform," as is being advocated by insurance companies, drug companies, and other large businesses whose careless mistakes can cause serious harm or death, benefits wrongdoers and penalizes innocent victims. When a person is injured by another person's negligence resulting in, for example, paralysis, loss of a limb or eye, a traumatic brain injury that leaves him or her in a permanent vegetative state or severely mentally disabled, or severe disfigurement leaving him or her unable to enjoy life as a normal person, tort reformers want to limit the amount of money the innocent victim can recover for his or her injuries. The main target of their efforts is at limiting the amount the victim can receive for "non-economic" damages, such as pain and suffering, loss of enjoyment of life, loss of comfort and society with the victim's loved ones, and loss of intimacy and sexual relations with the victim's spouse, domestic partner, or significant other.

In the United States, under a legal procedure that has generally worked well since the founding of our country, an impartial jury of one's peers has been entrusted with making the determination of how much is a fair and adequate award to the injured victim. The jury, after hearing all the testimony of witnesses, weighing all of the evidence, and deliberating among themselves, decides what is a fair and adequate award in a particular case. The innocent victim of another person's carelessness should receive the total amount awarded by the jury.

To place an arbitrary limit on the most money an injured person can recover for any or all types of injuries is unfair and takes the decision of how much a victim is entitled to out of the hands of the jury. Each case is unique and requires the testimony of the victim, his or her family members, medical experts, pain experts, psychiatrists and psychologists, and other specialists.

Suppose the father of a seven-year-old boy is paralyzed from the neck down in a car crash. How do you place a value on the father's pain and suffering of being trapped inside a body that doesn't work anymore, the loss of enjoyment of life, the loss of society and comfort? No longer will the father be able to play catch with his son, take him fishing, go camping, or do other typical father-son activities. There should be no arbitrary limit on how much the jury can award for any type of damages.

Tort reform affects the most seriously injured victims, those most in need—and deserving—full compensation. The decision as to how much money the innocent victim should receive should remain in the hands of the jury and not subject to any arbitrary monetary limitations that benefit only wrongdoers and their insurance companies and deny the injured victim or his or her heirs full and fair compensation.

PART IX:
LOOKING BACK AND LOOKING FORWARD

Personal injury has had an interesting past as far as legal practice areas go. Few areas of the law have been so misunderstood while making so much progress. As this area of the law continues to evolve, it's interesting to look at the changes, and think about what the future might hold and how these cases continue to shape our communities.

36 THE "HOT COFFEE LADY" AND "FRIVOLOUS" LAWSUITS

Everyone knows the story of Stella Liebeck and her cup of McDonald's coffee that was too hot. It's been repeated over and over and used as an example of the "frivolous lawsuit."

People look at Liebeck v. McDonald's Restaurants and hold it up as an example that society has become too "sue-happy" because, of course, she should have known coffee is a hot beverage. Of course it had to be a cash-grab, and she was looking to squeeze a large corporation and make that payday we all dream of.

Well, hold on for one second. There's more to the story.

As it turns out, Ms. Liebeck spilled the coffee on her lap, which caused third degree burns over most of her legs and groin. She required a number of painful skin graft surgeries, and was disabled for a period of time.

The other part that tends to be left out of the anecdotal retellings of the story is the part where McDonald's served her coffee they knew was dangerously hot because they had been told repeatedly to stop serving coffee at near-boiling temperatures.

Not only that, but Ms. Leibeck was not the first person to be severely burned by McDonald's coffee. In fact, there were 700 reports of serious burns related to their coffee prior to hers.

What about that part where Ms.Liebeck "sued for millions of dollars?" Also not entirely accurate.

Ms. Liebeck initially asked McDonald's for $20,000 to cover her medical bills and lost wages. McDonald's offered her $800. After retaining a lawyer, Ms. Liebeck offered a settlement of $90,000, no questions asked, end of story. McDonald's also refused that and another settlement of $250,000 was offered at a settlement conference.

McDonald's had already settled other scalding claims for upwards of $500,000.

When the case went to trial, Ms. Liebeck was again seeking nothing more than compensation for her medical bills. It was the jury who awarded her $200,000 in actual damages and added the $2.7 million in punitive damages. This was because the jury felt McDonald's had prior warnings and knew exactly of the dangers and harm their coffee would cause if it were to spill. It was the jury who, after hearing all the evidence, believed that this would be ample punishment. A judge later reduced the punitive damages to $480,000. After appeals, the two parties settled on $600,000.

Ms. Liebeck just wanted her medical bills paid. It was the jury that held McDonald's accountable for their actions by setting the high actual and punitive damage amount.

The public's perception of the Liebeck v. McDonald's Restaurants case was skewed because most people didn't have the whole story. When presented with the full scope of the case, most people's opinions change drastically. This was more than "my coffee is too hot, I think I'll sue." Her case centered around the negligence of serving coffee too hot after being told repeatedly not to because people were getting hurt. In lawyer speak, this is called "being on notice."

In the wake of Liebeck v. McDonald's Restaurants, a moral outrage over "frivolous lawsuits" has erupted, causing many injured parties to be hesitant to sue, despite being seriously injured. This campaign is spearheaded and financed by billion-dollar insurance companies and corporations who want nothing other than to keep consumers from having a way to check their power.

There's nothing wrong with holding a responsible party liable when you are injured due to their negligence. Thinking your lawsuit is "frivolous" just because of something you heard on TV could force you to deal with a life-altering injury on your own when you don't have to.

In the future, the effects of Liebeck v. McDonald's Restaurants could continue to skew people's perception of personal injury cases. When you're hurt and you're seeking compensation for expenses you incurred because of someone else's negligence, and someone who has no knowledge of your case accuses you of "looking for a fast payday," you might get discouraged.

It's important to remember the Liebeck case because it reminds us that detractors don't usually know the full story. Hopefully, in the future we will see more people looking to understand the entire story, rather than just a soundbite.

37 FORD'S PINTO FIASCO AND DEFECTIVE PRODUCT CASES

In 1972, Lilly Gray was driving her Ford Pinto when she was rear-ended by another car. Her Pinto immediately burst into flames, severely burning her and her 13 year old passenger, Richard Grimshaw. Gray later died of her injuries and Grimshaw required multiple surgeries over 10 years to recover.

Cars don't normally burst into flames just from being rear-ended, and further investigation revealed a design flaw in the Pinto.

As it turns out, even a minor rear-end collision would cause the oddly placed fuel tank to be pushed forward, and possibly burst. This also came with the risk of spraying fuel into the passenger compartment, as well as the risk of sudden ignition.

Ford was absolutely and completely aware of this fact, and sold the Pinto anyway.

Repairing this design flaw would have cost Ford a total of $45.39 per car. After crash tests revealed the flaw and engineers informed them of the cost to rectify the flaw, Ford declined to implement the changes in order to save money on production.

The ensuing court case, Grimshaw v. Ford Motor Company became one of the best examples of defective product cases in history. The idea of a company selling products they know to be dangerous or deadly is repulsive at best, but it happens. Corporations unfortunately continue to put their profits over the safety of the same people who buy and use their products. While many people would figure the Grimshaw case to be the shake-up we needed for safe consumer goods, it unfortunately was not. Actually, it's been getting worse.

In 2015, the Food and Drug Administration issued recalls for 32 different medical devices found to employ faulty designs. Some of these devices were implanted in people's bodies, where they failed and caused catastrophic injuries, turning people's lives inside-out. This was just in the medical field; consumer goods as a whole have been seeing more and more recalls for faulty designs.

Take for example, the Hoverboard craze. These self-balancing scooters seemed fun at first, until they started bursting into flame while people were riding them. A design flaw in the toys' batteries was causing them to overheat and ignite. What seemed like a fun ride at first ended up being a horror scene as people's Hoverboards were exploding under them.

There's nothing wrong with holding a manufacturer responsible for selling you a product they knew to be dangerous. Reluctance to do so goes back to the fallout from the Liebeck case, where people are fast to accuse plaintiffs of making a "cash-grab" when they were legitimately injured.

As we look back on the mounting piles of defective product claims, a question of accountability arises. If you don't hold these manufacturers responsible, who will? People have become reluctant to litigate because of the fear of being mocked in public.

Moving forward, it's important for you, the consumer, to do two things. First, you must conduct research. Has this happened to other people who purchased this product in the past, and are the cases well documented? Second, you must communicate openly with your lawyer. When you decide to seek legal representation, listen to your lawyer's advice. When it comes to cases like this, most lawyers will be very upfront with you regarding the value of the case. Lawyers don't like wasting your time or theirs, and if they tell you there's a case there, there's a case. If there wasn't, they'd be very clear that the case isn't worth the time to fight it.

38 CHANGES TO THE LAW

The law is an ever-evolving thing, and is constantly being updated and reinterpreted. Since the first edition of our book, there have been some changes to California's laws that pertain to personal injury. Other rulings have changed how the courts view certain kinds of damages.

These are just a few examples of how the law has changed in the short time since our First Edition.

Leung v. Verdugo Hills Hospital

This was an interesting case that has changed the way shared or joint-liability is handled.

In 2012, the California Supreme court reversed a lower court's decision, thus undoing a 200 year old concept regarding co-defendants and something called "good faith" settlements. With this decision, your lawyer has to change how they handle a case with more than one at-fault party. The change, however, benefits the victims in a major way.

Aidan Ming-Ho Leung was six days old when he suffered irreversible brain damage due to a mistake by his pediatrician. The case was complicated when it was revealed that the hospital was also at fault for not catching the preventable mistake, thus making the damage worse. Leung's parents sued both the pediatrician and the hospital, seeking to hold both parties responsible.

The pediatrician agreed to a settlement with the Leung family of $1 million, the limit of the malpractice insurance policy. The hospital, on the other hand, did not settle and took the case to trial.

A jury found the pediatrician 55% at fault and the hospital 40% at fault, placing 5% of the fault on the Leung family. Before damages were awarded, the hospital appealed the ruling on the grounds of a common law "release rule." This release rule stated that once a plaintiff settles with one co-defendant, the other defendant is off-the-hook, and cannot be held liable. The hospital used this rule to claim they could not be held liable for Aidan's brain damage, since the family had accepted a settlement with the pediatrician.

The California Supreme Court decided that the family in fact did have the right to seek compensation from the hospital, despite having already settled with the pediatrician. This created what is now called the "setoff-with-contribution approach."

After the Leung decision, if more than one party is responsible for your injuries, they both have to either answer to a jury or settle. If Party A decides to settle, Party B doesn't get to just walk away scot-free. This eliminates the "waiting game" some co-defendants can use: waiting to see if the other co-defendant settles before making their next move.

Sherman v. Hennessy Industries, Inc.

In 2015, the California Supreme Court declined to review this case, thus upholding a lower court's decision. What it did was protect workers from defective products they're forced to use.

Michael Sherman was a mechanic for Hennessy Industries, building drum brake pads. One of the machines employed in the manufacturing process was ejecting asbestos dust while in operation. Sherman was bringing the dust home on his clothes, which eventually caused his wife to develop mesothelioma, a disease she later died from.

Sherman sued his employer, arguing they failed to properly notify him of the machine's dangers and did not protect him fully. The employer argued they could not be held liable for a product they did not design or manufacture.

A jury initially ruled in favor of Sherman, and Hennessy quickly appealed. Hennessy argued again that they could not be held liable since they did not design the product, citing an earlier judgement. The courts found this to be an exception to the rule, since Hennessy knew the brake pads contained asbestos, that asbestos was harmful for you, and that the machine exposed workers to it.

Since the California Supreme Court would not review the case, this means that if you are exposed to a hazardous or faulty product, the party who placed you in that position can be held liable.

This has far reaching implications, since it removes protections from a number of situations. Imagine if a shopping mall uses an escalator they know is defective. Or if a car rental company rents you a vehicle previously shown to be faulty.

The "we didn't design it" defense no longer keeps you from recovering damages from someone who exposed you to danger.

Howell vs. Hamilton Meats Inc.

Many people don't realize that their medical care is often billed to their insurance provider at a substantial discount. You might rack up a medical bill of $70,000, but the hospital bills your insurance company at a discounted rate of $40,000 or so.

For a long time in California, this discount was ignored and a plaintiff would be awarded "fair market value" for the medical services rendered. While the hospital only billed for $40,000, you'd be awarded the full $70,000 in bills.

In 2011, the California Supreme Court made a landmark decision that changed all of this, in turn changing the entire face of Personal Injury law.

A woman named Rebecca Howell was injured in an accident caused by a truck owned and operated by Hamilton Meats Inc. When her case had gone to trial, she had received just short of $190,000 worth of billable medical care.

Howell's insurance company however, received a discount from the hospital, and only paid $60,000.

With the law the way it was then, when Howell won the case, the meat company had to pay the full $190,000 of medical costs. After the judgement, they appealed the decision and said they should only have to pay the $60,000 the insurance company was billed, since that's the actual amount that was paid.

After a long legal battle, the case ended up in front of the California Supreme Court, who sided with the meat company. They were only liable for the $60,000 the insurance company was billed.

This has effectively punished you for having insurance. You pay for your insurance to cover the costs of an injury, yet you are completely unaware that the hospitals are giving insurance companies such a discount. Nobody tells you this until it becomes vital information.

Howell vs. Hamilton Meats delivered a massive blow to the rights of accident victims. The California Supreme Court effectively endorsed the questionable practice of providing massive discounts to insurance companies as a way to cover themselves.

The Howell decision is basically insurance for the insurance companies.

Troy and Alana Pack Patient Safety Act of 2014 (Prop 46)

In the 1970s, the state of California placed a cap on the amount of money a plaintiff could be awarded in a medical malpractice suit. This meant that if someone was injured because of a doctor's mistake, they could only recoup $250,000 in damages.

Even in the 1970s, people had a misconception that plaintiffs in personal injury cases were looking for a payday. This, of course, is not true. The political climate didn't see it that way, however.

Fast forward to 2014, and the caps had not moved. While $250,000 may have been a substantial amount in the 1970s, it was nowhere near ample in the 2010s. The cost of living, inflation, changing medical climate, and other factors made that cap an absurdly inadequate amount. The cost of recovering from a major malpractice incident was several times that.

But the cap remained.

Prop 46 aimed to raise this cap, to give victims and their family a much more realistic settlement. While a system with no cap would make much more sense, the proposition was just a start. The cap was to be raised to $1 million, giving juries freedom to award appropriate amounts.

The proposition was defeated based on two things. First, the opposition argued that the bill wouldn't have been about protecting patients, but benefiting trial lawyers. The second issue hinged on pieces that were tacked onto the law regarding drug and alcohol testing for doctors and other such measures. Doctors were furious about this, as they felt it was an overreach by the government.

As the debate raged, the opposition kept repeating the idea that the law would only benefit "the greedy trial lawyers." Proponents of the bill insisted this was about getting victims awards that made sense.

Proposition 46 would have made sure you were compensated for all expenses and damages you incurred from a malpractice injury. It also would have held doctors who committed malpractice accountable for their negligence. Doctors would no longer be able to hide behind the caps and their malpractice insurance, but would be held financially accountable.

Yet over and over, it kept coming back to this idea of "greedy trial lawyers"—an idea firmly rooted in the stigma left over from the Liebeck case. People still, for some reason, felt like there was a wave of cash-grabbing lawsuits out there—an idea that is entirely fictional.

Because of the drug testing clause and the public's misconception of what these caps meant, Prop 46 is merely a memory.

This brings a chilling problem for the future. Malpractice cases aren't going to be worth fighting anymore.

With the damages capped at the 1970s level they are now, merely mounting and fighting the case costs more than you could ever be awarded. Too many lawyers will end up passing on these cases, since they'd end up being a Pyrrhic victory at best.

With Prop 46 defeated, will victims of malpractice ever get the justice they deserve? It's hard to say.

39 A QUICKLY APPROACHING AND UNCLEAR FUTURE

The world is a very different place than it was when we wrote the first edition of *Accidents Happen*. There are things in the world now that simply didn't exist then. Just as the record industry had to adapt their legal philosophy when streaming music services got started, there are plenty of new technologies that will change the face of personal injury law in the future.

Self-Driving Cars As Defendants

It sounds utterly absurd, but this is now a reality. Recently, one of Google's experimental self-driving cars struck a city bus in Mountain View, CA. While this wasn't the first accident involving a self-driving car, it was the first time the car was found to be at fault.

Yes, the car was at fault.

Because of the way the software recognized road hazards, the car moved to the left in order to avoid sandbags that were in front of a storm drain. This caused it to hit an approaching city bus. It was determined the car was at fault for not yielding to the bus. While thankfully there were no injuries, what if there had been? Who would be held liable?

It's a question with no clear answer at the moment. These self-driving cars are essentially robots, which of course are not people. So if the robot car is at fault and someone is hurt, can a robot be held liable? If not the robot, would you hold the company that made the car's software? It's not like they could have planned ahead for that specific situation, since the car navigates on a series of decision-making algorithms and not pre-loaded scenarios. What about the person in the car? Should they have taken over the controls? What if the car malfunctioned?

Nobody as an answer for what to do about these self-driving cars in case of injury accidents. Ultimately, Google will most certainly have responsibility, but lots needs to still be developed in this new area of the law.

Are Uber Drivers Employees?

Uber is an interesting beast. The ride-sharing service allows people to use their own cars almost like a taxi service. Except that it is very much not a taxi service, since the cars are not owned or operated by Uber and are private vehicles. The drivers simply give rides to people in their car and are compensated for their time.

So what happens when that goes wrong?

In 2014, a Los Angeles woman accused an Uber driver of "abducting" her. After picking her up, the driver took her 20 miles out of the way, ignoring her as she told him this was the wrong route, finally stopping in an empty parking lot and locking the doors. As the woman shouted for help, the driver eventually drove her home, ending the two hour ordeal.

A case in the California courts about a year later established Uber drivers as actual "employees" after a former Uber driver sued for job-related expenses. This classification is not nationwide, however. Other states have ruled differently, and some haven't had to rule at all yet.

This is going to begin coming into question more and more as the ride share service becomes more widespread and common. As convenient as Uber and other similar services are, who is liable when things go wrong? Do we have to just hope the driver carries insurance? Should Uber be providing insurance? If the driver is providing their own insurance, should the insurance policy treat passengers like any other passengers or correct for them as "customers"?

These questions are all up in the air right now, as the growing pains of the industry begin to iron themselves out. Many lawyers are keeping a close eye on these cases to see how they play out.

Complicating the matter is the issue of drivers with a checkered past. How thoroughly is Uber required to check the backgrounds of its drivers? Since they're a type of independent contractor, is Uber liable if they miss something? Even if the driver's record is clean, what if they commit a crime while on the job? As an independent contractor, does the blame lie solely on the driver?

Drone Flights On Public And Private Property

Unmanned Aerial Vehicles (UAVs) or "drones" have come out of nowhere and are becoming a huge legal issue.

Of course, there's the "invasion of privacy" question that comes with any remote controlled vehicle that carries a camera. This is a question as old as the invention of binoculars. Yet, the drone question is deeper than that.

In 2015, a fire broke out on the 15 Freeway near the El Cajon Pass, north of Fontana, CA. Cars were stopped on the freeway as multiple vehicles burned right there on the road, including a boat trailer and a car carrier. As fire crews attempted to put the fire out, their efforts were hindered by private drones that were in the area as locals tried to film the fire.

These drones made it almost impossible for the fire crews to bring helicopters into the area to drop water and fire retardants on the burning vehicles. Since, at the time, the FAA hadn't required registration for drones, nobody knew who the pilots were.

Should these drone pilots be held liable for keeping firefighters from doing their jobs? Should they have to pay for the damage to cars that were burned? What if there were injuries?

What about certification? Should some sort of training and certification be required before someone can fly a drone? If an unlicensed drone pilot causes property damage or personal injury, how does that change the case? If they're licensed and operate the drone in an unsafe manner, would this mean they're especially negligent?

As the law evolves and changes, more of these questions will need to be asked. It won't be easy, and like any other process of change, there will be bumps in the road. However, it's worth noting that we've come through changes and questions in the past to get to where we are now. It's not too much to imagine that we'll figure it out from here as well.

AFTERWORD

As you can see from either reading this whole book or just the chapters that apply to your situation, persons who have been seriously injured or killed due to another person's carelessness ("negligence") or a defective product are entitled to fair and adequate compensation for their injuries or their loved one's death. Money does not replace an amputated limb or cure paralysis due to a severed spinal cord, but it is the only way we have of making the person "whole" again.

This book discusses many common ways that you may be injured or killed, as well as many of the injuries and damages you may suffer due to another person's negligence. To discuss all of the ways in which you may be hurt by another's carelessness or deliberate conduct and the injuries you could suffer would take up several volumes.

If you have been seriously injured or a loved one killed due to another person's negligence, in addition to getting timely medical attention for your injuries, you should contact an experienced personal injury lawyer as soon as possible. The lawyer will want to begin an immediate investigation into the cause of your injuries to see whether another person, product manufacturer, or governmental entity is responsible for your injuries. The lawyer can also assist you in getting the proper medical care for your injuries and damages, and get fair and adequate compensation for a loved one's death.

If you have been injured or a loved one killed in an accident, you should consult an attorney quickly before evidence is lost or destroyed or witnesses move from the area or their memories of the accident fade. Also, you may be required to file a claim with the appropriate agency within six months—or even shorter—of the incident or your right to sue the guilty party will be lost forever. Don't guess about your legal rights or the value of your case. Protect yourself and your family and promptly retain an experienced law firm that can properly and effectively represent you.

Reza Torkzadeh
Allen P. Wilkinson

ABOUT THE AUTHORS

REZA TORKZADEH is an award winning attorney who has dedicated his entire career to representing individuals and their families in serious personal injury and wrongful death cases. Reza has been named on the US World News & Report Best Lawyers list for 2015, 2016 and 2017. He has been recognized on the Super Lawyers list every year since 2010, and listed as a top 40-Under-40 Trial Lawyer as recognized by the prestigious National Trial Lawyers Association every year since 2012. Reza is an invited member of the Multi-Million Dollar and Million Dollar Advocates Forum, one of the most respected invite-only plaintiffs' attorney organizations in the country. He obtained one of the largest personal injury verdicts in the country in 2015 and continues to fight for the protection of consumers against insurance companies and corporate defendants.

ALLEN P. WILKINSON was admitted to the California State Bar in 1979. He started his legal career by working for the legendary San Francisco trial lawyer Melvin Belli for 10 years. With Mr. Belli, Allen wrote the popular consumer book Everybody's Guide to the Law in 1986, for which Allen did a completely revised and updated second edition in 2003, published by HarperCollins. Allen has written extensively for the legal profession and is a highly regarded legal writer. He currently lives in Laguna Woods, California, where he concentrates on legal writing and consulting with personal injury lawyers and law firms.

INDEX

15-passenger vans 57–58, 205

A

absolute liability and aircraft accidents 177

accident reconstruction experts 3, 33, 42, 45, 47, 79

accidents. see specific types and causes of accidents

accidents, definition of 179

accidents, reporting of 61–62

accident scenes 24–26, 33

activities of daily living 207, 225

actual notice 57, 111

adjusters, insurance 35, 42, 62–63

aggressive driving 55, 73

aircraft accidents 165–181

air traffic controller errors 170

alcohol 55, 57, 66, 73, 89, 93, 103, 104, 107, 108, 156, 244

amputations 223–228

Amtrak Reform and Accountability Act 84

amusement park rides 141–150

Answer, definition of 44

appeal, right to 48

arbitration 15, 43

asbestos 135, 154, 257

assumption of risk inherent in a sport 153–157, 159, 163

automatic warning devices 87

automobile accidents 12, 41, 53–64, 130,197, 229

aviation law 165–181

B

BAC (blood alcohol content) 55, 75, 92

baseball 153–154, 159–163

basketball 151

beyond a reasonable doubt 4, 45

bicycles

    accidents 97–102

    bicycle lanes 98–99

    motocross (BMX) 158–159

Bill of Particulars 186–187, 191

blood alcohol content (BAC) 55, 75,92

BMX (bicycle motocross) 158–159

boating and personal watercraft accidents 106–110

bone grafts 199–200

bones, broken 197–200

bouncy castles. See inflatables

boxing 152

breathing difficulties 204

broken bones 197–200

bungee jumping 157

burn injuries 214–222

Bush, George W. 75, 85

C

California Civil Code 118, 125

California Division of Occupational Safety and Health 143

California Supreme Court

    appeals to 49

    Howell vs. Hamilton Meats 258

    on common carriers 68, 118,145–146, 148

    on inherent risk of a sport 151–155

    on joint-liability 255

    on pain and suffering damages 235

California Vehicle Code 98, 100

capsizing 108

car accidents 21, 53–64

carbon monoxide poisoning 107, 216

care, standards of. see highest standard of care; limited duty of care; ordinary standard of care

carelessness. see negligence

carnival rides 141–150

casts 198

causes of accidents, investigations into 21–22

cell phones 55, 83

central nervous system 201

chair lifts 156

chemical burns 217

children
bicycle helmets 99
comparative negligence 122
dog bites and attacks 126
under DOHSA 190
escalator accidents 122
pedestrian accidents 104
wrongful death cases 12

civil law xix

Clinton, Bill 84

Cockpit Voice Recorders 171

Colgan Air accident (2009) 172

collision insurance 61

collisions 53–64, 71–72, 92, 97

Comair accident (2006) 172

combination-unit trucks 71

commercial airplanes 167–181

common carriers
amusement rides 144–148
chair lifts 156

commercial airplanes 167–169
definition 68
elevators and escalators 117–120
highest standard of care 68
passengers' rights 67–69
passenger trains 82
public transit 66

commuter planes 172

comparative fault 5, 135

comparative negligence
children under 5 122
definition of 5
dog bites and attacks 126
large truck accidents 81
motorcycle accidents 95
pedestrian accidents 105
slip/trip and fall injuries 115
train accidents 90

Complaint for Damages 44

component products 134

consortium, loss of 189
see also pain and suffering

construction sites 121

constructive notice 57, 112, 188

consumer expectation test 133

Consumer Products Safety Commission (CPSC) 143

Continental Connection Flight 3407 172

contingency fee agreements 36–37

contracts/tickets 160, 183–188, 191

contributory fault 178–179

contributory negligence 5

CPSE (Consumer Products Safety Commission) 143

criminal law xix

crossbucks 87

cross-examination 47

crossing gates 87

crosswalks 103, 104

cruise ships 182–192

D

damages

  aircraft accidents 174–175

  automobile accidents 60, 237

  broken bones 200

  burns, 173

  comparative fault 5

  cruise ship accidents 185

  under DOHSA 189

limitations of in medical 138

malpractice cases 242–243, 260, 107–8

for pain and suffering 232–236

in personal injury cases 9–11

PTSD 230

TBIs 209

value, determination of 28–29

in wrongful death cases 12–16

DCA (District Court of Appeal) 48–49

Death on the High Seas Act (DOHSA) 180–181, 183, 189–192

Death on the High Seas Amendment (2000) 181

deaths. see fatalities

Default Judgments 44

defective design or manufacture 78, 96, 99, 130–136

de-icing 170

Delta Connection accident (2006) 172

demand letters 43

dependents and wrongful death cases 12

depositions, definition of 44

depression 196, 204, 209, 211, 228, 229, 230

dermabrasion 220

Dermagraft-TC 221

design defects 78, 96, 99, 124, 130, 132, 133, 158, 170

discovery, definition of 44

disease on cruise ships 183

Disneyland 141, 144–147

District Court of Appeal (DCA) 48

diving 155, 205

dog bites and attacks 125–129

DOHSA (Death on the High Seas ACT) 180, 183, 189–192

domestic flights 173–175

driver distraction or error 53–54, 66, 73, 99, 103

driver fatigue 73, 74–75

drivers, independent truck 79–80

drones 263–264

drowning 107, 182

drugs and accidents 56, 57, 66, 73, 99, 103, 109

due care. see highest standard of care; ordinary standard of care

E

economic damages

aircraft accidents 179–180

cruise ship accidents 185

definition of 10

under DOHSA 181, 189

medical malpractice cases 138

TBIs 212

train accidents 85

elderly and pedestrian accidents 103–105

electrical burns 217

elevator injuries 120–121

escalator injuries 121–122

evidence, gathering of 33

excessive preventable danger 133

exculpatory clause (express releases of liability) 159

excursions from cruise ships 183, 188

exemplary damages 16, 179

expert witnesses 3, 36, 45, 47, 139, 158

explosions on cruise ships 183

express releases of liability 101, 159–160

F

FAA (Federal Aviation Administration) 170–173

failure to

inspect the premises 112

maintain vehicle in proper operating condition 76, 79

yield the right-of-way 99

falls 111–116, 205, 207

falls overboard 108

fatalities

aircraft accidents 165, 167, 174, 180–181

automobile accidents 53, 56, 58

bicycling accidents 97

boating and personal watercraft accidents 107, 109

burns 216

cruise ships accidents 183

dog bites and attacks 127

large truck accidents 71–73, 75

motorcycle accidents 92–93

pedestrians 104

SCIs 202, 205

see also wrongful death

fatigue, driver 73, 74–75

fatigue and TBIs 209

fault. see liability

Federal Aviation Administration (FAA) 170–173

federal courts and train accidents 85

Federal Employers Liability Act 89–90

Federal Motor Carrier Safety Administration 75

15-passenger vans 57–58, 205

fires on cruise ships 183

flammable materials 73

"Flight Crew Techniques and Procedures that Enhance Pre-takeoff and Takeoff Safety" (FAA), 173

Flight Data Recorders 166, 171, 172

food poisoning 182

football 152, 153, 205

forensic accountants 45

foreseeable uses 133

form SR-1 62

fractures 196, 197–200

fraudulent insurance claims 54

freight trains 82–83, 85–86

friction burns 93, 98, 105, 216

G

Golden Rule argument 234

golf 154–155

grief and sorrow 10, 15, 174, 190, 228, 233

gross negligence 158
see also negligence

gymnastics 205

H

Hague Protocol 176

hazardous materials 73

head-on collisions, truck 72

hearsay 59

heat inhalation burns 73, 215

heirs and wrongful death cases 14–15

helicopters 169, 264

helmet laws 94–95

hemicorporectomy 223

highest standard of care
amusement rides 145–148
children and, 91
commercial airplanes 169
common carriers 68–69
mass transit 67, 68–69
passenger trains 82

high seas, definition of 181

hockey 205

hold harmless contract (express releases of liability) 159

holding oneself out to the public 148, 168
see also common carriers

horse-drawn stagecoach ride (Disneyland) 146

horse racing 152, 153

horse riding 157, 159

hot air balloons 169

I

IATA (International Air Transport Association) 177

ice hockey 205

implied notice (constructive notice) 57, 122, 188

improper use of product 132, 135

independent truck drivers 79–80

Indiana Jones ride (Disneyland) 144–145

infections 198, 206, 215, 221, 227

infectious disease on cruise ships 183

inflatables 141, 143, 148–149

inhalation burns 73, 215

inherent risk of a sport 151–156

injuries

civil law and xix–xx, 3

comparative negligence 5, 11

survival actions 13

the trial process 44–49

valuation of 9–11, 17–18

see also specific type or cause of injury

inspection

of airplanes 166

of amusement rides 143, 147

of boats and personal watercraft 109

of elevators and escalators 121, 123

instrument flight rules 166

insurance and insurance companies

adjusters 35, 42, 62–63

aircraft accidents 174

boating and personal watercraft 110

collision 57

fraudulent claims 54

medical malpractice 138–140, 256

motorcycle 94

reporting accidents 61

settlements 44

uninsured motorist coverage 59–60

intentional misconduct 101, 151, 159

Intercarrier Agreement (1996) 177

International Air Transport Association (IATA) 177

international cruises 184

international flights 175–180

J

jackknifing 77

judgments and uninsured or underinsured motorists 59

juries 13, 15, 18, 45–48, 139, 232–236, 241–246

L

landlords and dog bites and attacks 129

lane splitting/sharing 93–94

large truck accidents 71–81

lawsuits, progress of 44–49

lawyers

aviation accident 174

medical malpractice 138–139

selection of 33–35

settlements without 62–63

see also personal injury lawyers

leash laws 128

liability

airplane accidents 169, 170, 175–179

amusement rides 145–146

boating and personal watercraft accidents 108

clarity of 18

comparative negligence and 5–6

contributory fault 178

cruise ship accidents 184, 186–187, 188, 191

determining 3

dog bites and attacks 125–126

elevator and escalator accidents 116–117, 120, 123

impairment and 55

inflatable accidents 148–149

large truck accidents 79–80

mass transit accidents 65, 66, 68

police reports and 22

of railroad companies towards employees 89–98

rear-end collisions 54

releases of 101, 157, 159–160,

strict product liability 124, 131, 134, 170

train accidents 82, 89

license suspensions 75

lifejackets 107

lights, bicycle 100

limited duty of care 153

Los Angeles Dodgers 162

Los Angeles Kings 163

loss of consortium 189

loss of enjoyment of life

  broken bones 199, 200

  burns 222

  cruise ship accidents 185

  definition of 10

  limitations of in medical
    malpractice cases 138,
    242, 244

  pain and suffering 232, 234

  psychological injuries 230

  TBIs 213

  value, determination of
    17, 45

loss of services 13

lost wages and earnings 5,
  9–10, 13, 16, 17, 43, 55, 58,
  63, 85, 90, 158, 175, 200,
  213, 222, 250

M

maintenance of equipment or
  vehicles 66, 73, 76–77, 121,
  123, 141, 144, 170, 182

major depressive disorder 230

manufacture, defects in 78,
  99, 130, 132, 134

maritime law 188–192

mascots 163

mass transit accidents 65–70

mechanical problems 73, 76,
  78, 143, 169132

mediation 43

medical expenses 10, 13, 17,
  46, 63, 138, 242

Medical Injury Compensation
  Reform Act of 1975
  (MICRA) 138

medical malpractice xvii, 3,
  137–140, 232, 241, 259

Metrolink accident (2008)
  82–84

MICRA (Medical Injury
  Compensation Reform Act
  of 1975) 138

mild traumatic brain injury
  208

minors
  see children

mobility devices 226

moderate traumatic brain
  injury 209

monetary value see value of a
  case, determination of

Montreal Agreement (1996)
  176–177

Montreal Convention (1999)
  177–180

Motion for Nonsuit 47

motorcycle accidents 92–96, 216

motor vehicle accidents see automobile accidents, motorcycle accidents

mountain climbing 154

mule trains (in California) 147

municipal transportation accidents 65–70

N

National Highway Traffic Safety Administration (NHTSA) 77, 94, 103,

National Transportation Safety Board (NTSB) 84, 166, 174

negligence

airplane accidents 167, 170, 180

amusement ride accidents 142, 144

auto accidents 57

boating and personal watercraft accidents 107, 108

broken bones 200

burns 218

comparative 5, 11, 122

contributory 5

definition of xx, 166

design of course 158–159

in design of products 131

elevators and escalators 118, 119, 123

entrustment 60

gross negligence 101

large truck accidents 79–80

mass transit accidents 68

medical malpractice and 137, 138

pedestrian accidents 105

per se 128

railroad crossing accidents 88

release from 101, 157, 159

sports 151, 156

negligent entrustment 60

NHTSA (National Highway Traffic Safety Administration) 77, 94, 103

NTSB (National Transportation Safety Board) 84, 166, 174

non-economic damages

aircraft accidents 179

definition of 10–11, 15

DOHSA 181, 190

limitations of in medical malpractice cases 138, 242–245

for pain and suffering 232–136

train accidents 85

non-passengers 66, 69, 82, 123

non-pecuniary damages. see non-economic damages

Norfolk Southern Railroad accident 86

NTSB (National Transportation Safety Board) 84, 166, 174

O

Obama, Barack 85

occasional sellers 131

Occupational Safety and Health, California Division 143

one-time sellers 131

operator carelessness 66

ordinary standard of care

businesses 112

commercial airplanes, 130

cruise ship accidents 183

definition of 69

non-passengers 66, 82, 123

non-passenger trains 82

pedestrian accidents, 79

private carriers 166–168

public transportation 66, 69

spectators at sporting events 161

other motorists, unsafe 80–81

P

pain and suffering

aircraft accidents 175, 179, 181

automobile accidents 55, 58, 63

broken bones 199

burns 222

comparative fault and 5

cruise ship accidents 185, 190

limitations of in medical malpractice cases 138, 232, 242–245

non-economic damages 10, 17, 45, 232–236

survival actions and 15

TBIs 213

train accidents 85, 91

pain management 224–225

paralysis. see Spinal Cord Injuries

paraplegia 98, 150, 201–206

passengers

airplane 167, 173–175, 177

automobile 57

boat 107, 108

cruise ship 181–182

elevators and escalators 118, 119

mass transit 65–69

motorcycle 93

railroad crossing accidents 88

train 82–85

Uber 263

passenger trains 82–85

pecuniary damages see economic damages

pedestrian accidents 103–105

per diem rule 235

permissive user statute 59

personal injury cases. see damages

personal injury lawyers

amusement ride injuries 150

automobile accidents 60, 63

burns 222

cruise ship accidents 186

selection of 33–35

slip/trip and fall injuries, 89

train accidents 89

uninsured or underinsured motorists 60

personal watercraft accidents 106–110

phantom pain 224

photographs and accidents 33

physical assaults by cruise ship crew members 183

pilot error 159, 170

Pirates of the Caribbean ride (Disneyland) 146

pit bulls 127–128

plaintiffs 14, 29, 45–48, 161, 234–235, 253, 256, 259

Plus Three/Minus Eight rule 171

police reports 22, 59

positive train control (PTC) 84

Posttraumatic Amnesia (PTA) 209

Posttraumatic Stress Disorder (PTSD) 196, 211, 229–230,

prejudicial errors 48

preponderance of the evidence 3, 45

pre-trial settlement conferences 45

private airplanes 165–166

private carriers 166

products, defective 3, 130–136, 252–254

proof, standards of 3, 45, 131

prostheses 224–228

proximate cause xx

psychological injuries 10, 175, 185, 229–231
    see also Posttraumatic Stress Disorder

PTC (positive train control) 85

PTSD (Posttraumatic Stress Disorder) 196, 211, 229–230

public entities
    large truck accidents 78
    mass transit accidents 65–70
    motorcycle accidents 94
    negligence by 57
    railroad crossing accidents 86

railroad workers' accidents, 89

time limits in filing claims against 41, 69, 96

public interest and express releases of liability 160

public transportation
    see mass transit accidents

punitive damages 16, 85, 177, 179, 250

Q

quadriplegia 201–206

R

racing 56, 152, 158

radiation burns 217

railroad crossing accidents 57, 86–89

railroad workers 89–91

raw materials suppliers 134–135

rear-end collisions xx, 3, 53, 252

reasonable care towards employees 90

rebuttal witnesses 47

recalls, product 132, 253

recklessness and express release of liability 159

recreational sports injuries 151–159, 205

reduction of bones 198

Reeve, Christopher 202

reflectors 100

regional jets 172

registered owners 57, 59–60, 61

remanding of case 49

reporting of accidents 22, 61–62, 107, 109, 143, 185

respondeat superior 79

responsibility see liability

right-of-way, failure to yield 54, 55, 80, 99, 261

risk-benefit test 133

road conditions 73, 99, 103

rock climbing 159, 160

roller coasters 142, 144, 146

rollover accidents 58

roofs, crushed 56, 58

Rottweilers 127

rugby 205

rules of the road and bicyclists 98–99

runway incursions 170–171

runway errors 173

S

sabotage 170

Safety Alert for Operators 173

scars 219–221

SCI (Spinal Cord Injuries) 58, 105, 142, 149, 183, 201–206, 265

SDRs (Special Drawing Rights) 177–178

sea, aircraft crashes at 180–181

services, loss of 13

settlements
  aircraft accidents 174
  cruise ship accidents 187
  good faith 255–256
  McDonalds coffee suit 250
  multiple plaintiffs 14–15
  personal injury lawyers 35, 36–37, 42, 60, 28, 33–34, 46
  pre-trial 45
  without lawyers 63–64

severe traumatic brain injury 142, 209, 210

sexual assaults by cruise ship crew members 183

shaken-baby syndrome 144, 208
  see also traumatic brain injuries
side trips from cruise ships 188
single-car accidents 57
skiing 156, 205
skin grafts 220–221, 249
slip and fall injuries 111–116, 130, 182, 207, 212
small claims court 48
smoke inhalation 216
snowboarding 156
snow skiing 156, 205
soft tissue injuries xviii, 62, 195
Special Drawing Rights (SDRs) 177–178
spectators, injuries to, 125–27
speeding, 56
Spinal Cord Injuries (SCIs) 58, 105, 142, 149, 183, 201–206, 265
sports and sports injuries 151–164, 205
  see also specific sports
Sports Utility Vehicles (SUVs) 56, 57–58, 72, 205

spouses and wrongful death cases 12
SR-1 form 62
standards of care. see highest standard of care; limited duty of care; ordinary standard of care
state courts and train accidents 85
street racing 56
strict liability and aircraft accidents 178
strict product liability 131
suicide 56, 204, 205, 228, 250
surfing 205
survival action suits 13, 16, 190
survivors and wrongful death cases xvii, 12
SUVs (Sports Utility Vehicles) 56, 57–58, 72, 205
swimming 182
systemic toxin burns 215

T

TBIs
  see traumatic brain injuries
Teamsters Union 75
thermal burns 214

tickets/contracts 160–162,
183–188, 191
time limits
aircraft accidents, 140–41
cruise ship accidents 183,
186–187
under DOHSA 191
large truck accidents 78
mass transit accidents 69
motorcycle accidents 96
public entities, claims
against 41
railroad crossing accidents
89
railroad worker's accidents
90
tort law, definition of xix–xx
toxin poisoning 215
train accidents 82–86
traumatic amputations 223
traumatic brain injuries (TBIs)
about 207–213
from amusement rides
142, 149
automobile accidents and
58
bicycle accidents and 98
cruse ship accidents and
182

elevator accidents and 120
motorcycle accidents and
95
pedestrian accidents and
105
traveling carnival rides
143–144
trials, progress of 44–49
trip and fall injuries 111–116,
120, 182, 207
trivial defects and slip/trip
and fall injuries 113–115
truck accidents 71–81
truck drivers, independent
79–80
turning, large trucks 77

U

uninsured or underinsured
motorists 57, 59–61, 237,
244
United States Supreme Court
on definition of an accident
179
U.S. Consumer Products
Safety Commission (CPSC)
143.
used goods 131

V

value of a case, determination
of 17–18, 42–43, 254

vans, 15-passenger 57–58, 205

vehicle maintenance, failure of
66, 73, 76

veterinarian's rule 129

vicarious liability 79

visual flight rules 166

W

waiver agreement (express
releases of liability) 159

Warsaw Convention (1929)
175

watercraft, personal accidents
106–110

water skiing accidents
108, 109

weather conditions 25, 56, 78,
108, 166

wheelchairs 9, 10, 226

whiplash 63, 195–196,
208, 252,

Whiplash-Associated Disorder
196

wholeness and damages xx

witnesses 22

cruise ship accidents 186

expert 3, 36, 45, 47, 139,
158

rebuttal 47

slip/trip and fall injuries
and 116

testimony 47, 145

timeliness of selection of
lawyers 33, 42

worker's compensation 89, 121

wrestling 205

written release of liability 157

wrongful death 10, 12–16, 28,
86, 102, 105, 165, 176, 188